# ADVANCE PRAISE

"The story of Ed Hale would fit neatly into one of the rags to riches books by Horatio Alger. He is an example of the can do attitude that quickly propelled America to the pinnacle of the economic world. He is a personal friend who has benefitted Baltimore greatly."

— Benjamin S. Carson Sr., MD

Emeritus Professor of Neurosurgery, Oncology, Plastic Surgery and Pediatrics, Johns Hopkins Medicine

President and CEO American Business Collaborative, LLC

"I've known Ed for years as a friend, neighbor, businessman and advisor—at least I thought I did. Even longtime associates will see Ed anew after reading this candid and insightful biography of a real Baltimore legend. Ed is a brilliant visionary willing to take on projects no one else believes possible, most often with great success. But at the heart of Ed's often wild and outrageous stories is a man who feels truly compelled to leave his community better than he found it. This book confirmed for me what I have always known about Ed Hale: expect the unexpected."

— Dutch Ruppersberger, U.S. Representative

# HALE STORM

The Incredible Saga
of Baltimore's Ed Hale,
Including a Secret Life with the CIA

# HALE STORM

The Incredible Saga
of Baltimore's Ed Hale,
Including a Secret Life with the CIA

## KEVIN COWHERD

Apprentice
House Press
Loyola University Maryland

First Edition

Printed in the United States of America

Hardcover ISBN: 978-1-62720-035-6
Ebook ISBN: 978-1-62720-036-3

Design by Apprentice House
Cover photo by Karen Jackson

Published by Apprentice House


Apprentice House Press
Loyola University Maryland
4501 N. Charles Street
Baltimore, MD 21210
410.617.5265 • 410.617.2198 (fax)
www.ApprenticeHouse.com
info@ApprenticeHouse.com

It is not the critic who counts; not the man who points out how the strong man stumbles, or where the doer of deeds could have done them better. The credit belongs to the man who is actually in the arena, whose face is marred by dust and sweat and blood, who strives valiantly; who errs and comes short again and again; because there is not effort without error and shortcomings; but who does actually strive to do the deed; who knows the great enthusiasm, the great devotion, who spends himself in a worthy cause, who at the best knows in the end the triumph of high achievement and who at the worst, if he fails, at least he fails while daring greatly. So that his place shall never be with those cold and timid souls who know neither victory nor defeat.

— Theodore Roosevelt

# Contents

ACKNOWLEDGEMENTS .....................................................xi

FOREWORD BY MARYLAND
  GOVERNOR MARTIN O'MALLEY .............................1

INTRODUCTION.................................................................3

CHAPTER 1: "He was just an average good kid" .................9

CHAPTER 2: Starting slow, dreaming big...........................19

CHAPTER 3: The Break of a Lifetime .................................25

CHAPTER 4: You snooze, you lose .....................................31

CHAPTER 5: The Midas Touch Redux................................39

CHAPTER 6: No Business for the Weak ..............................45

CHAPTER 7: Trouble in Shangri-la.....................................53

CHAPTER 8: A Judgment for the Ages................................61

CHAPTER 9: The Wizard of Oz Buys a Team .....................71

CHAPTER 10: "Mom, I have All These New Friends" ......87

HALE THROUGH PHOTOS...............................................99

CHAPTER 11: Fresh Air Comes With a Price .................117

CHAPTER 12: The Agency Comes Calling......................123

CHAPTER 13: Back in the Game .....................................135

CHAPTER 14: "We Built This Bank For You."................149

CHAPTER 15: Working Hard, Playing Hard....................157

CHAPTER 16: A Tower Rises From the Wasteland.........167

CHAPTER 17: The Saga of Girlie Hoffman ....................173

CHAPTER 18: Living on Top of the World......................177

CHAPTER 19: The Fixer ..................................................185

CHAPTER 20: Storm Clouds on the Horizon .................191

CHAPTER 21: "The Deepest, Darkest Bowl of Crap."....201

CHAPTER 22: Still Going for the Action.........................207

ED HALE'S LIFE LESSONS............................................215

AUTHOR'S BIOGRAPHY...............................................219

# ACKNOWLEDGEMENTS

As legions of journalists can attest, interviewing Ed Hale is an experience like no other.

His cell phone rings incessantly. Or it beeps with a fresh text or email from business connections, attorneys, friends or family members. If you're talking to him in his Rosedale office, his long-time secretary, Cindy Smith, might buzz to tell him about a call waiting on his land-line or a package that recently arrived. Or she'll whisk silently into the room with budget figures for him to examine or papers to sign.

All of it commands his immediate attention, because Hale would rather drive a nail through his eyeball than miss a timely message that could lead to his next business deal or the next great adventure in his life.

Nevertheless, he was unfailingly gracious during these interruptions and extremely generous with his time throughout this project.

All told, we talked for nearly 75 hours about his life. We talked about everything from his modest upbringing in eastern Baltimore County, the ups and downs of his incredible business career and his hitherto-unrevealed service with the Central Intelligence Agency to the rocky periods of his two marriages, his relationships with his three children and the bevy of beautiful women he'd dated over the years.

We talked in restaurants, fast-food joints, bars and coffee shops. We talked at his home in Miller's Island, with its spectacular views of the Back River, Middle River and Chesapeake Bay. We talked in a rain-soaked duck blind as he hunted with friends on his 186-acre farm in Talbot County.

(As a biographer, you haven't lived until you've conducted an interview with shotguns blasting around you, hunters whooping deliriously, the smell of spent shells wafting through the air and waterfowl dropping from the skies like doomed warplanes in battle.)

We talked on a crowded MARC train returning to Baltimore from Washington D.C., where we had met with his former CIA handler, David Miller, and Steve Kappes, the former Deputy Director of the agency, to go over what we could include in the book about Ed's years of service there.

We talked in his luxury automobiles as we zipped along the streets of Highlandtown, where he was born, and Sparrow's Point and Edgemere, where he grew up. We talked outside Pot Spring House, the historic Timonium mansion in which he once lived, and on walking tours of Canton, where his vision helped transform a bleak landscape of toxic waste sites, coal ash and rotting piers into a vibrant slice of Baltimore waterfront.

We talked on several occasions in the Baltimore Blast locker room, once after a disheartening loss and right before coach Danny Kelly delivered a brilliantly profane and hilarious (well, if you weren't a player) dressing-down of his team that threatened to peel paint off the walls and leave little old ladies in the hallway in shock.

This does not include the hundreds and hundreds of texts we exchanged from April of 2013 until the fall of 2014.

(A personal favorite: on a morning when I was whining about

some family obligation I was dreading, Ed texted to let me know his day wasn't shaping up so great, either: "Fucking beautiful! I'm goin' to my tax accountant and then to get my prostate checked. Yeah, baby!!!"

(Thus confirming that for a biographer, there is no such thing as too much information.)

For all the candor Ed showed, all the cooperation he provided, all the access he gave to family members and friends, and all the contact information he provided about those who played a significant role in his life, both good and bad, I am deeply grateful.

Others who cheerfully offered their assistance and gave of their time in the making of this book include:

Bill Atkinson, Kevin Atticks, Marty Bass, Karen Bokram, Barry Bondroff, John Buren, Edie Brown, Dick Crane, Larry Crane, Scott Dorsey, Dr. James D'Orta, George Duncan, Mildred Edling, John Eisenberg, Salvatore "Soccer Sam" Fantuzzo, Ashley Elizabeth Flamholz, Jim Gast, Alexandra Hale, Bonnie Fleck, Barry Hale, Buddy Harrison, Kevin Healey, Henry Hopkins, Jennifer Gilbert, Carol Hale, Phil Jackman, Ken Jones, Melvin and Ruth Kabik, James Kallstrom, Michele Kearns, Blast coach Danny Kelly, Dan Kelly, Jim Kraft, Harvey Kroll, A.B. "Buzzy" Krongard, Drew Larkin, O. James Lighthizer, Harry Lipsitz, George Mantakos, Dickie McGee, Bob Meehan, Sen. Barbara Mikulski, Judge Joe Murphy, Kevin O'Connor, Kevin O'Keefe, Dottie O'Neill, Gov. Martin O'Malley, Joe Poiter, Ty Pruit, Rep. C. A. Dutch Ruppersberger, the all-knowing Cindy Smith, Department of Transportation secretary James Smith, Shale Stiller, Douglas Schmidt, Tony Tranchitella, Sheila Thacker, Mark Wasserman, Mike Watson, Gregg Wilhelm and John Williams.

My thanks and eternal gratitude to all.

Kevin Cowherd
September 2014
Cockeysville, Md.

# FOREWORD

## BY MARYLAND GOVERNOR MARTIN O'MALLEY

Ed Hale's amazing story is one I've followed since my earliest days on the Baltimore City Council, when he was already a force in the community, a leading entrepreneur and banker with a passion for helping his hometown.

And help it he did. The people who make this world a better place and the people who create wealth and create opportunities and reclaim abandoned areas, they're the people who have the ability to see what it can actually be. And more than that, have the courage to risk action on the faith that they can make it so.

And that's one of the things I've always loved about Ed Hale. Win or lose, he steps up to the plate. He swings at the pitches. And he hits a lot of them. And people can talk about the ones he didn't hit, the ones he swung at and missed. But the fact of the matter is, the guy makes his own bat. He did not wait for anyone else to make it for him.

For a lot of people in Baltimore, Ed Hale represented a sort of Everyman. Folks saw that the guy could be their brother. They thought: he *did* build this bank for me—that was more than just another soul-less corporate slogan when Ed started and nurtured 1st Mariner.

But from the very beginning, Ed was always more than just another CEO. What people crave in these times of large failing institutions and large fumbling government is the authentic person. Somebody who actually lives the American Dream. It's not something that we'll take our children to see only in museums or talk about how, in another generation, people used to work hard, sweat, work three or four jobs, risk it all, fail, pick themselves up, try again, succeed, succeed more greatly, fail, succeed again.

That's what America's all about. I think there are a lot of people in Baltimore—and I'm certainly one of them—who admired the guts and courage and unrelenting optimism that Ed Hale threw at life every single day.

And now when I go down to Canton to see the places that Ed built, see the properties that he got rolling and onto the tax rolls, see the number of young people that think it's hip and cool to live in the city again, it's a pretty remarkable transformation in a short period of time. And Ed was a pioneer down there.

Now, in this engaging biography by author and former Baltimore Sun columnist Kevin Cowherd, Ed's story comes to life. It's all here, from his modest upbringing in Sparrow's Point to his wildly-successful careers in trucking, shipping, banking and real estate to his ownership of the Baltimore Blast and championing of indoor soccer, his secret work for the CIA, his often-turbulent family life and the difficult business setbacks he weathered later in his life.

As you'll see, it's a story well worth telling.

# INTRODUCTION

You wonder what Hollywood would do with a story like Ed Hale's.

You wonder if they'd screw it up, focus only on the power and wealth, the women and the expensive toys, and miss the essence of the man: the chip on his shoulder the size of a sequoia that drives him, the business wizardry that seems hard-wired in his DNA, the lust for action and competition and the work ethic that made him a bootstrapping folk icon in his hometown of Baltimore.

Still, you figure a big-shot movie producer would happily set fire to his Maserati to get a script like this: scrappy kid from a working-class enclave who couldn't hack community college goes on to hit it big in trucking, shipping, banking and real estate.

A millionaire before he's 29, he pals around with members of Congress, governors and mayors, buys a pro soccer team, lives in an historic mansion that once housed the Duchess of Windsor and later in a 10,000-square-foot tower penthouse that looks like the Ritz Carlton, entertains Saudi princes on his luxury yacht and is the only man in history known to have turned down a dinner date with the achingly beautiful actress, Halle Berry.

A larger-than-life figure, he knows only one way to think, and that's big.

A dozen years ago, he looks at 22 acres of forlorn brownfields and rotting wharves along the Baltimore waterfront and announces plans to build a $1 billion complex, including an office tower, condos, stores and restaurants.

The critics tell him he's nuts, it'll never work, you couldn't get people to go down there if you held a gun to their heads. But today the area is thriving, a civic jewel overrun with hordes of yuppies and hipsters who drop $30 for crab cakes without blinking an eye and prattle on and on about their favorite craft beers and artisanal wines. And the Shops at Canton Crossing, the area's new outdoor mall, is generating millions of dollars in revenue, forever preserving his legacy as a genuine hometown visionary.

Oh, and there's also this: it turns out that at the very pinnacle of all this success, he's secretly working for the Central Intelligence Agency, in on the ground floor of the early hunt for the arch-terrorist, Osama Bin Laden.

And that's just the bare outline of the story of Edwin Frank Hale.

The American Dream? The man didn't just chase it. He bear-hugged that sucker and dragged it to its knees, lived it better and more fully than most men ever will.

Of course, any story about Ed Hale worth its salt would have to chronicle the dark times, too. And there were plenty of those.

Even as his various business empires grew, his home life was often tense and chaotic, sad and dysfunctional.

"I was a terrible husband and a terrible father," he says in a typically self-lacerating assessment of his failed attempts at domesticity.

Both his marriages broke up, at least in part, because of his infidelities and workaholic tendencies, and he fathered two children out of wedlock. With ex-wife no. 1, he was on the losing end of the biggest divorce settlement in Maryland history. And when it was clear he was going down in flames, he tried to stick it to her attorney by paying his court-mandated fee of $277,000 in small coins.

Determined to keep unions out of his trucking and barge businesses, he got so many death threats he started packing a .38-caliber Smith & Wesson, hired a bodyguard and wore a flak jacket at public events. He even looked into buying a bullet-proof car built like a tank, but balked when told it got only six miles to a gallon of gas.

There were multiple business setbacks, too, misfortunes so profound his friends thought he belonged on suicide watch.

He lost millions when a truck dealership he owned went belly-up. Years later, he lost many millions more and was left empty and saddened when he stepped down as chairman and CEO of his beloved 1st Mariner Bank, the "neighborhood bank" that foundered during the housing crisis and had federal regulators circling like vultures.

And when he couldn't obtain permanent financing and had to sell the iconic 17-story 1st Mariner Tower --- the one he built that helped transform the blighted Canton waterfront into East Baltimore's "Gold Coast"—another little piece of Hale's soul seemed to go with it. As did another huge chunk of his bank account.

In the midst of it all, he survived three plane crashes. After one, in which he splashed down in the Chesapeake Bay at the height of his squabbles with the Teamsters and International Longshoreman's Union, a former FBI supervisor urged him to have the engine tested to see if it had been tampered with.

The test came back negative. But Hale was only slightly comforted, subscribing as he does to the theory famously articulated in Joseph Heller's brilliant anti-war satire "Catch-22": "Just because you're paranoid, doesn't mean they're not after you."

Someone, it seems, was always after Ed Hale: union goons, divorce attorneys, bank regulators—even the angry ex-boyfriends of some of the stunning young women he dated over the years. And along the way there was a strained relationship (to put it mildly) with his father and bitter feuds with his three children, other family members, former business associates and friends that often lasted for years.

"He doesn't just burn bridges, he stomps on their embers," says long-time friend A. B. "Buzzy" Krongard, the former head of the venerable investment firm Alex. Brown & Sons and former executive director of the CIA.

"He's the best friend you could have—and he'd be the worst enemy," says Edie Brown, the veteran Baltimore publicist who has known Hale for decades or since, she says, "he was poor."

But if you had a friend in Ed Hale, you had a friend for life—especially during the bad times.

Go ask Bill Eyedelloth, a longshoreman and one of Hale's hunting buddies, about Hale's kindness and generosity toward his pals when they're down.

Four years ago, Eyedelloth is working a crane at the Port of Baltimore when he's overcome by a stabbing pain at the base of his skull. The pain worsens until his head feels ready to explode. He waves off worried pleas from co-workers to let them call an ambulance. Instead, barely able to focus, he somehow drives himself to University of Maryland Upper Chesapeake Medical Center in Bel Air, where his wife, Cathy, once worked as a nurse.

The doctors examine him. The diagnosis shakes him to his very core: brain hemorrhage.

"Call Ed," Eyedelloth gasps to Cathy from a gurney in the Intensive Care Unit. "He'll know what to do."

Hale gets on it right away. He makes a few calls, arranges to have Eyedelloth transferred to Johns Hopkins Bayview Medical Center, with its top-notch neurology and neurosurgery units. Eyedelloth spends 10 excruciating days in a haze of painkillers as doctors monitor the healing of a "vein bleed" in his brain.

On the day he finally gets word that he won't need surgery, 15 of his worried family members are gathered at the hospital. Hale is there, too. He promptly offers everyone the use of his condo to shower and freshen up, then takes them all out to dinner in Little Italy and picks up the tab.

Ken Jones, a former vice-president of Hale's trucking firm, is another who can tell you what it's like to have Ed Hale in your corner during a crisis.

When Jones' dad is dying of cancer in 2000, Hale comes to him one day and says: "Pick out a Saturday." Hale knows Jones' dad likes to gamble. But Hale also knows a long car trip to Atlantic City would be too much for the old fellow at this late stage of his illness.

So Hale puts his plane and pilot at Jones' disposal. And on a glorious weekend morning, Jones, his mom and his sick dad fly from Martin State Airport in Middle River up to Atlantic City.

The old man has the time of his life and wins five grand playing the slots and blackjack. And when the three arrive back at the plane for the return flight home, there's champagne chilling in an ice bucket, courtesy of Ed Hale, to cap off the day.

"My dad talked about it for the next month or two before he finally passed," Jones said. "It was the high point of his life."

Hale's fierce sense of loyalty to those he's close to is why Maryland Congressman C.A. Dutch Ruppersberger calls him a "foxhole friend."

"In politics, you're up, you're down," Ruppersberger said. "But it seemed Ed would always be with you when times were tough or times were good. But if you weren't his friend, watch out. I think he saw almost everyone as an adversary."

Yes, there's that side of Ed Hale, too.

He remains, at 67, a polarizing figure. For every one who speaks glowingly of his accomplishments, there's another who wants to push him down a flight of stairs. As with many wealthy and powerful individuals, allegations of unsavory business practices have dogged him throughout his career. Over the years, he gained a reputation as a tough, ruthless businessman with a penchant—at least early in his career—for suing at the drop of a hat. (For the record, he won the vast majority of those suits.)

"If I had an 800-lb gorilla sitting on Ed and a .45 at his head, he'd still be telling me he'd kick my ass," said John Arnscott, who bought Hale's dying Peterbilt truck dealership years ago after a series of tooth-and-nail negotiating sessions.

Proud, impatient, demanding, profane, vain—sure, he's had a little work done on his face, which he's not secretive about—Hale is all of those things, too. Like many who have achieved enormous success in life, he's a complicated man.

He's also funny, thoughtful, well-read, a life-long Democrat with a finely-honed sense of social justice who nevertheless espouses traditional Republican ideals of lower taxes, curbed entitlement programs and wariness of government intrusion in the free market.

Long ago, he bleached almost all traces of a "Bawlmer" accent from his speech in order to appear more worldly in his business dealings. He arranges dried flowers and has designed the interiors of both his homes, not to mention the exterior of the distinctive 1st Mariner Tower that rises from the Canton landscape like the jutting finger of God.

Yet his humor can veer to the sophomoric and the scatological, especially when he's hunting with his buddies on his Easton, Md., farm or off on fishing trips to the pristine lakes of northern Canada.

(This much is certain: in the history of modern civilization, no one has derived more pleasure—and gotten more laughs—from a $14.50 fart machine than Ed Hale.)

Friend and foe alike marvel at his energy levels, work habits, ability to juggle a dozen different projects at once and refusal to be intimidated by the doubters and nay-sayers that have watched him from the sidelines throughout his career.

His first wife, Sheila Thacker, calls him an "unstoppable force."

This, then, is his story.

On second thought, Hollywood may want to take notice after all.

# CHAPTER 1

## "He was just an average good kid"

Hanging on one wall in Ed Hale's Rosedale office is a telling document, framed and displayed behind glass like a museum piece.

It's his original sixth grade report card for the 1957-1958 school year at Edgemere Elementary. Sprinkled with mostly B's and C's, it also contains a note from his teacher, Joe Waurin.

It is not the sort of note that would make a parent's heart soar.

"I wish you would speak to Edwin concerning his behavior in class," Waurin wrote. "For the past few weeks, it has been very bad and his attention in discussions has been bad also."

Carol Hale wasted little time in responding.

"I am sure you will see a change in Eddie," she wrote. "Both his father and I were very ashamed to hear this."

Translation: I will smack him upside the head so hard his *kids* will be born with a headache. You will have no further problems with the little monster. That's a promise.

Hale displays the report card as a self-deprecating memento and a connection to his roots more than anything else. But maybe it also foreshadowed how the eternally-restless boy was loathe to conform to the dictums of others and destined to take a different path in life.

He was born in the blue-collar Baltimore neighborhood of Highlandtown on Nov. 15, 1946, the oldest of five children. The noisy birth took place on the third floor of his grandparents' house for the most practical of reasons: money was tight and there was often no room across the street at City Hospital, where the Baby Boom of the post-World War II years was in full flower.

His father, Edwin H. Hale, was a Navy war veteran and cable splicer for Baltimore Gas & Electric, born and raised in Lynn, Mass. His mother was the daughter of a Baltimore City Fire Department captain, Frank Feehley.

When Eddie was 6 years old and his brother Barry was 3, the Hales moved to Sparrow's Point in Baltimore County, in search of grassy spaces where the kids could play. They settled on a bungalow across from the Sparrow's Point Country Club and not far from Bethlehem Steel Corp., the mammoth shipbuilding and steel-making plant that dominated the area in the years following the war.

From all accounts, the neighborhood was a fine place for a kid to grow up. The area was populated with the young families of steel-workers, lured by the prospect of steady jobs and affordable housing. There was no shortage of friends for the Hale brothers, who were soon joined by identical twin sisters Jean and Jane, and a younger sister, Robin. The back yard, ringed by a chain link fence, became a gathering place for the neighborhood children and the site of countless ball games of all sorts.

Little Eddie played well with others—at least outside the house. But it took him a while to adjust to the idea that he'd be sharing living space with siblings and would no longer be the sole subject of his parents' attention.

When Barry was born, Hale recalls with a chuckle: "I thought 'Who is *this* guy? And what's he doing in *my* house?' He'd be lying in the crib and I'd look around"—to make sure no one was watching— "and I'd go *pop*. Give him a little jab."

Once, when Barry was taking a bath in the lone bathroom in the house, Ed came in to use the toilet. Unfortunately for Barry, the toilet was directly adjacent to the bathtub. As Eddie was standing there going about his business, he suddenly shifted—"like the turret of a tank turning," Barry recalled—and began urinating on his younger brother.

Another time, when the two boys were older and both were scrambling down the stairs to see who could get to the bathroom first, Eddie settled the matter by simply peeing on Barry through the banister railings.

But revenge was sweet. Later that day, Barry crept up behind a sleeping Eddie with the stealth of a mob hit-man and whacked his brother in the head with a hammer.

"He had just pissed in my face!" Barry recalled. "I could plead insanity."

From an early age, the Hale kids were taught the value of hard work, self-sufficiency and contributing to the common good of the family. Barry Hale recalls his father blasting John Phillip Sousa marches from the stereo on Saturday mornings, banging a pot with a wooden spoon as he marched through the house cheerfully bellowing: "GET UP! WE HAVE CHORES!"

Eddie Hale did whatever he could to make a buck: washing cars, mowing lawns, painting houses, scrubbing floors, babysitting the neighbors' kids. In the summer, he dove into the creek at the country club to retrieve golf balls, then sat at the front gate and sold them back to the golfers, many of whom he caddied for. In the winter, he recalled, "I would literally sleep in my clothes when it was snowing, so I could be the first one out in the morning to shovel and make money."

"He was just an average good kid," Carol Hale said. "We demanded respect and that (the children) be seen and not heard. We insisted that we all had dinner together, and we went to church together."

By the time young Eddie was in grade school, his grandfather, Frank Feehley, had become a major—and beloved-- influence in his life.

A combat veteran of World War I who served with an artillery unit in France, Feehley encouraged the boy to read anything he could get his hands on—even the labels on soup cans—and to be open and inquisitive about all aspects of life.

Eddie, in turn, basked in all the attention his grandfather bestowed upon him and was transfixed by his stories of life in the fire department and the legendary blazes he and his men had fought.

"That's no indictment of my father," Hale says now. "My father had four other kids to worry about. He was scrambling around, working hard, working extra hours to make money."

So it was Feehley who took Eddie to his first Orioles game, a 7-0 loss to the Cleveland Indians at Memorial Stadium. There the boy was mesmerized by the shimmering, immaculately-manicured green grass, so different from the scruffy brown fields he had played on at Edgemere Elementary School.

It was Feehley who stoked Eddie's love of trains by taking him down to Erdman Avenue to watch the trains rumble past, laden with passengers or cargo and bound for distant, exotic places the boy could only imagine. And it was Feehley, a volunteer at the Veterans Administration hospital at Fort Howard, who persuaded a doctor to let Eddie examine blood samples under a powerful microscope, spurring an interest in microbiology that would last for years.

When Eddie was 15, his grandmother in Massachusetts got him a job at Camp Najerog, a summer camp in Vermont run by a man named Harold "Kid" Gore. It was to be a major turning point in his young life.

Kid Gore was a charismatic, regal-looking figure. A former basketball, football and baseball coach at the University of

Massachusetts, he wore white, pressed linen outfits, a white duck-billed cap and held court in an Adirondack chair in front of the main house, his Dalmatians at his feet and the campers gathered around him.

Eddie Hale worked in the camp's kitchen, a job he described as "washing dishes and pots and pans for rich kids." At first he was painfully self-conscious of his working-class background and Baltimore accent, and of the few well-worn clothes and possessions he'd brought along.

"They definitely looked down on me," he said of the campers. "It definitely frames who I am.... They had everything I didn't have."

But after a couple of weeks of camp, Kid Gore took him aside and said: "I've watched you play ball. You're a good athlete. You should play tennis."

Coming from the worldly camp director, this was music to young Eddie's ears. It motivated immediately. "It was the first time in my life anyone had ever shown confidence in me," he recalled.

He took to tennis with a passion and soon was beating kids who had practically grown up with a racquet in their hands. It was an enormous ego boost for the small, skinny kitchen boy who had felt so out of place weeks earlier.

(Tennis would go on to play a major role in his life. He would play at Sparrow's Point High School his senior year with little distinction. "Never won a match. Never won a set. I don't think I won a *game!*" he recalled. But he kept working at the sport, eventually becoming accomplished enough to play at Essex Community College and then for the Homeland "A" team, a top amateur squad in Baltimore, for many years of his adult life.)

When he wasn't working or playing tennis at Camp Najerog, he fished in a cool, clear mountain lake nearby that was ringed by magnificent pine trees. The setting was a far cry from the gray, heavily-polluted waters off Sparrow's Point where Hale and his friends would catch what he called "fish with warts."

On his first outing on the lake, he caught the biggest fish anyone would catch that summer, a monster 19-inch bass. Soon, his industrious nature and athletic prowess earned him a much-coveted "Stout Fellow" cheer from the entire camp, led by the great Kid Gore himself:

"Boom boom, bang bang,

"Crack crack, pop pop!

"Camp Najerog, tip top!

"Yay Ed, yay Ed, yay Ed!"

Yet a day later, when Eddie violated camp rules and was caught in the kitchen after-hours with his face in a bowl of ice cream, a disappointed Kid Gore reacted as if the boy had stabbed a fellow camper.

"I wish I could take back that cheer," Gore said with a sad shake of his head.

But it was too late for that. Eddie Hale was becoming a camp standout. And by the time he returned home to Sparrow's Point, his self-esteem had been thoroughly turbo-charged.

"I found out that these kids from privileged backgrounds weren't any better than me," he said. "They weren't any better at tennis, and they weren't any more intelligent that I was, either."

The encouragement from Kid Gore only deepened Eddie's sense that he wasn't getting enough support and recognition at home, especially from his father. He also began to chafe at what he saw as the elder Hale's truculent nature.

"The stuff my father would say, the negative stuff, drove me," he said.

On family car trips, when a song by rock n' roll pioneers Elvis Presley or Bill Haley and the Comets came on the radio, young Eddie would pipe up from the back seat: "Isn't this cool!?" But invariably, he says, his father would shake his head and mutter: "Rock and roll is never gonna make it."

And when Eddie played YMCA football as a scrappy but under-sized lineman in the 14-16 age division, he remembered his father saying, referring to a couple of neighborhood kids: "Why can't you play like Fuzzy Lomax and Jesse Owens?"

"These were older guys with, like, mustaches!" Hale says now. "They probably had *kids*, too! It was like my father was embarrassed at the way I was playing. You know what that does to your self-esteem? I remember thinking: I will *never* be like him."

To this day, though, Barry Hale and his sisters Jean and Robin—Jane died of breast cancer in 2004—remain mystified by Hale's resentment toward his father, who died in 2002. The rest of the Hale siblings insist Eddie was treated no differently than anyone else in the household by a loving, hard-working father trying to raise five children amid growing financial pressures.

"We often wonder what family Ed grew up in," Barry Hale says of Ed's perception of their father. "The house was a happy home!"

Nevertheless, Eddie's discontent with his home life was very real. He was so unhappy at times that he began doing financial calculations on the total cost of his upbringing, with the idea of paying his parents back and never speaking to them again. In addition, he hatched elaborate plans to run away from home on a raft, Huck Finn-style.

At one point during his teenage years, the boy who never shied away from work also didn't shy away from another way to make a buck.

When an older kid in the neighborhood offered $15 to anyone who would steal four spinner hubcaps for a 1957 Chevy, 15-year-old Eddie Hale leaped at the opportunity.

On a cold winter night, he snuck out of his house. Along with a friend named Leroy Grey, he canvassed the streets until the right car was found. The hubcaps came off easily. With each boy carrying two, they decided to split up.

But the two were not exactly master criminals.

Right away, Eddie Hale violated rule no. 1 for those engaged in the legendary shady enterprise known as Midnight Auto Supply: don't walk around with the stolen goods in plain sight.

First, a drunk in a pickup truck spotted the skinny kid carrying two shiny hubcaps at 2 in the morning. He chased Eddie and grabbed him from behind, and both slipped on the icy sidewalk. Somehow, Eddie whacked him with a hubcap and took off.

But the get-away was an unmitigated disaster, too.

Hiding behind swamp grass in Bear Creek, he fell through the thin ice up to his ankles. Wet, shivering, with cuts and bruises all over his body, he hid the hubcaps behind a gas station and walked home.

Just as he pulled up to the house, though, so did the cops. They threw him in the back of the squad car and took him back to where he'd tussled with the drunk, now being tended by paramedics. In a scene right out of a sitcom, the beered-up man, grimacing in pain, somehow raised himself from his stretcher when he spotted Eddie and cried "That's him!" Then he was taken away in an ambulance with neck and back injuries.

Eddie was hauled down to the Dundalk police station and tossed in a cell. His father was called to get him. Not surprisingly, the senior Hale was not in a swell mood after being awakened in the middle of the night to retrieve his son, the budding young hoodlum.

"I have all I can do to keep from mopping up all of Dundalk with you," he said to the boy, who fully agreed a beating would be justified.

Things did not get a whole lot better for Eddie Hale the next day.

His father insisted that he go to school, despite his late-night "crime spree" and the fact he was working on about two hours sleep. Later that morning, he was summoned over the loudspeaker to the principal's office. On the way, he noticed several police cars parked in front of the school as well as a familiar-looking '57 Chevy.

"I'm a dead man," Eddie thought.

D-E-A-D.

At the very least, he imagined a stint in reform school in his immediate future, with the possibility of all sorts of violent sexual assaults on his person. With the principal and the cops and the car owner staring balefully at him, Eddie Hale caved like a mineshaft and admitted to the theft.

But when the cops asked the Chevy owner if he wanted to press charges, he shook his head and said no.

"Look at him, he's all beat up," the man said, pointing at the boy. "Just give me my hubcaps back."

"The man was smart enough and decent enough to realize it was just a kid making a stupid mistake," says Hale now. Young Eddie apologized profusely, returned the stolen items and promptly ended his life of crime for good.

Years later, when invited to speak at the commencement exercises for the graduating class of the Baltimore County police academy, Hale would tell the story of his early brush with the law and joke: "If I'd been successful, I probably would have been the Tony Soprano of Maryland."

But real-life crime czars had a knack for ending up behind bars or in a cemetery with a weeping parent's tears dampening their headstone. Even at a young age, neither of those prospects held any allure for young Eddie Hale.

As a headstrong kid growing up in a large, boisterous family where money was tight, he was looking for *something*.

But the life of a bad guy definitely wasn't it.

Eddie Hale had much bigger plans.

# CHAPTER 2

## Starting slow, dreaming big

By his senior year at Sparrow's Point High in 1964, a sense of despair gripped Ed Hale as he contemplated a future of limited possibilities.

"It was a feeling almost bordering on desperation," he would say later. "'Cause I knew I hated school and didn't want to go to college. Only about 10 per cent of our graduating class went to college anyway. It was just assumed you were going to work at the steel mill or be a laborer. Or be drafted and go off to Vietnam and get killed."

The summer after graduating from high school, he worked at Beth Steel in the open hearth and blast furnace. It was a tough, dirty, otherworldly atmosphere that left him awestruck and wondering how anyone could drag themselves out of bed every morning and work there year after year after year.

"The absolute heat and violence of what was going on there, the size of these buckets of molten steel!" he recalled. "They would tap the furnace with dynamite and there would be this big explosion! Sparks would fly all over the place and you're standing there! I worked in something called the mold yard. They would pour liquid steel so it could be transported into these sand frames and they would dump this stuff. And if there was spillage, I'd go in and shovel up the rocks or clean up the sand out of these molds."

The heat was stifling and danger was ever-present.

"And I wasn't savvy enough to realize: one misstep and you were dead. There was always this story: 'Did you hear about Bill? Bill fell into the bucket (of molten steel) and was vaporized!' So they would dip out some of the steel, a brick of it, and give it to his family for burial.

"People got their arms and legs cut off. I'm 19, working in the blast furnace, working underground in something called the stock house. The stock house feeds this conveyor, a little automated train car that would go by slowly and noiselessly. And I'd have to throw rocks in this train car as it passed me. And it's 2:30 in the morning, obviously you're not in the right frame of mind. And I'd be backed up to this train car and it would hit me every once in a while. And if you got hit and you fell backward rather than forward, you'd get cut in half."

But it was also while working in the blast furnace that Eddie Hale arrived at an epiphany about the direction his working life would take—or *not* take.

"I'd be standing there," he recalled, "and they'd have these trenches where molten steel would come down. It would be stuff called slag."

Slag was stony waste matter separated from metals during the smelting or refining of ore.

"And the slag would still be glowing and they would send us in there with big sledge hammers to break it up and then shovel it into containers to take away. And your feet would burn. You'd put car tires—you know, like retreads from trucks?—on your feet so they wouldn't get blistered. Once your feet got hot, they never cooled off—ever.

"The whole time I'm thinking: 'I'm never working here. *Never*. I don't care how much money they pay me. I gotta do something. I don't know what it is. But I gotta do *something.*"

He decided to give college a shot after all, enrolling at Essex Community College in February of 1965. First he had to take remedial courses in math and English at Dundalk High School in order to be accepted. But except for playing tennis and ogling pretty girls, not much about undergrad life appealed to him, even though he had vague—and unrealistic—aspirations of someday being a doctor.

That same year, he started dating a girl named Sheila Thacker. She was a funny, artsy, black-haired beauty who was a dead ringer for Cher Bono, just emerging as a pop-singing sensation with the husband-wife duo Sonny & Cher.

Sheila was a senior at Patapsco High in Dundalk. At a Halloween party at her house, a girlfriend introduced her to Ed Hale, who proceeded to put the moves on her. They were not, both parties agree, the smoothest ever recorded in the history of romance.

"He had seen me around—I had caught his eye," Sheila recalled with a laugh. "He spent the night talking about what a great tennis player he was and how he had this red Austin-Healey sports car."

"I was still this little twerpy guy," Hale says sheepishly. "I had no game, no bullshit with girls. I was actually fairly shy."

In May of 1966, after two desultory years at Essex, Ed Hale enlisted in the Air Force to avoid getting shipped off to the jungles of Vietnam. Still entertaining thoughts of a career in medicine, he signed up to be a medical corpsman.

But a few months before he was to report to basic training in Amarillo, Tex., he was playing in a tennis tournament in Vermont when he received a phone call from Sheila. She had big news: she was pregnant.

The bulletin left 19-year-old Ed Hale reeling. He nearly dropped the phone.

"The range of emotions (was) all negative," he recalled. "There was no upside to me getting married. I'm going in the Air Force, she's pregnant, I don't know how I'm going to support her, where she's gonna live . . .

"But I knew I had to do the right thing. I *had* to marry her. 'Cause that's what was typically done back then."

The next day, anxious and confused, with a thousand thoughts swirling around in his head, he headed home to break the news to his parents and contemplate his future. Barreling down the Connecticut Turnpike in a '58 Dodge with rear fins so sharp they could slice meat, he wracked his brain for a way out of his predicament.

"I thought: 'You know what? Maybe I *won't* face the music,'" he remembered. "'Maybe when I cross the George Washington Bridge, I'll just keep heading west and go right to Texas.'"

Instead, he picked up a hitch-hiking sailor headed for Philadelphia and decided to continue on to Baltimore. He arrived at his parents' house at mid-afternoon on a Sunday, during a family cook-out. The news that their son was about to become a father did not sit well with Edwin and Carol Hale, who seemed, in equal measures, appalled and embarrassed.

"I really thought at that point that my life was over," Ed said. "I thought: 'I will never get out of this.'"

Ed and Sheila were married Aug. 25, 1966 at a church in Winchester, Va. Ed continued to work at Beth Steel for a few months, then worked for the ironworkers union until leaving for the Air Force in November.

Eddie Jr. was born Feb. 3, 1967, while Ed was away, and lived with Sheila at her mother's house in Dundalk. After basic training, Ed was given his choice of assignments and settled on Westover Air Force Base in Chicopee, Mass, where Sheila and the baby soon joined him.

By this point, Hale had become so adept at tennis that he was chosen for the team that would represent the base in tournaments. It was not an awful way to serve one's country: donning a polo shirt and shorts and hitting a fuzzy white ball over a net at the base country club, then retiring for a few drinks. And the tennis team traveled and played in some of the most beautiful locales all over the U.S.

But soon new orders arrived, signaling an end to this idyllic life.

Airman First Class Ed Hale was being assigned to Tan Son Nhut Air Base outside of Saigon. It was the height of the Vietnam War. Although he had no way of knowing it, in just a few months the air base would become a major target of the Viet Cong and North Vietnamese army during the fierce military campaign known as the Tet Offensive.

"I thought it was a death sentence," Hale said of his new assignment, and his spirits sank.

Like many of his generation back then, he was opposed to the unpopular war, skeptical of the so-called "Domino Theory" espoused by President Lyndon B. Johnson that all of Southeast Asia was in danger of falling to the communists. He was also deeply mistrustful of the motives of Secretary of Defense Robert McNamara and the "old dudes" sending young men off to battle for what seemed like a senseless cause.

Two of his classmates at Sparrow's Point High had been killed in Vietnam less than five months after graduation. And while he didn't see himself as a coward, the prospect of returning with missing limbs or in a flag-draped coffin unnerved him.

But fate soon intervened, in the form of a health emergency suffered by his young wife.

The couple learned that Sheila needed an extensive gall-bladder operation and would be laid up for some time, unable to work and earn money. One-year-old Eddie Jr. needed to be cared for, too.

Ed requested and was granted a hardship discharge from active duty. The upside: he would not be huddling under enemy rocket fire on the sun-baked airfield at Tan Son Nhut after all.

Looking back on it now, he says: "I think the discharge saved my life."

In August of 1968, he left the Air Force, facing a decidedly unsettled future.

For a time, he worked at Eastpoint Formal Menswear and Topps department stores, grumbling about the long hours and low pay. But anyone who knew Ed Hale knew that he wasn't long for selling tuxedos to pimply-faced prom goers or toiling in the dreary aisles of a discount chain.

"He had aspirations to big things," Barry Hale said. "Ed was always dreaming. Dreaming big."

And those dreams would soon become a reality.

# CHAPTER 3

## The Break of a Lifetime

In August of 1968, Ed Hale found himself working on a desolate lot in White Marsh renting truck trailers to Giant Food and Food Fair for a company called BDOW. It was an acronym for Best Deals on Wheels, which sounded like a used-car dealership staffed with smooth talkers in loud plaid sports jackets selling clunkers with rolled-back odometers. Mercifully, Hale was soon able to convince management to change the name to Atco Trailer Co., which by comparison sounded a thousand times classier.

Glamorous the Atco job was not, unless you found working in a hot 10-foot-by-40-foot office trailer with a balky toilet that had to be pumped from the outside enchanting. There was also this dubious perk: the weed-choked property was crawling with snakes.

Though just a clerk, Hale thrived at the business. He inspected the trailers, made sure the tires were properly inflated, did everything from billing and inventory to cutting the grass.

But some months later, fed up with making just $125 a week, he put in his two-week notice. He planned to take a job with Sea Land, the shipping and containerization company, which was offering him $200 a week.

What unfolded next, he maintains, was "the most important thing that happened to me in my life."

When he arrived for work the next morning, the owner of the company, Tony Tranchitella, was waiting for him.

Tranchitella was a decorated World War II combat pilot who had flown 66 missions in the Pacific Theatre. A dapper man who favored stylish suits and snazzy cufflinks, he was usually behind the wheel of a late-model Cadillac.

Now he had driven down from company headquarters in New Jersey to talk to his hard-working young employee.

Hale was flattered.

"Don't open up yet," Tranchitella said. "Let's go get some breakfast."

The two ended up at the Little Chef Restaurant on Pulaski Highway. The boss got right down to business. He wanted to know why Hale was leaving.

Hale replied that he had a job offer that paid $75 more a week. With a wife and 1-year-old son at home, he needed every penny of it. Plus he was peeved that he hadn't received bonus and commission money promised to him when he had first taken the job.

Money was so tight for the Hales that a kindly couple Ed had recently met, Mel and Ruth Kabik, had put up the $1,000 settlement fee when he went to close on his first house in Pikesville.

("That was so important!" Hale would say years later. "No one had ever given me anything like that." Mel Kabik, a former Marine who had fought in the South Pacific in World War II and who ran Eddie's Supermarkets and later branched out into real estate, would remain a life-long friend and confidant.)

Tranchitella listened patiently as Hale unburdened himself and said: "I don't want you to leave. You *get* it. You understand the business."

In the next breath, he offered to put Hale in charge of the lot and raise his pay to $200 a week, plus two per cent of the gross. The cash register in Hale's head whirred silently and his eyes widened.

"Holy shit! I'd be making $18,000 a year instead of $6,200!" he thought. (By comparison, a salary of $18,000 in 1968 would be the equivalent of nearly $125,000 today.)

"Ed was flabbergasted," recalled Tranchitella shortly before his death in 2013 at the age of 92.

In fact, Hale was so stunned that his fork froze over his sausage and eggs as he stared at the older man, wondering if he had heard right.

He had.

Before leaving, though, Tranchitella left his young employee with an onerous task. He wanted Hale to tell the manager he was replacing, a man named Rudy Paycik, that he was now being transferred to company headquarters in Berlin, N.J.

Paycik was a former Marine who fancied himself a bad-ass and carried a .45. He was also known to have a volcanic temper. Predictably, he exploded when a nervous Ed Hale passed along the message, accusing the young man of going behind his back and not letting him know the big boss was in town.

"I was prepared to take a beating," Hale recalled of that moment.

Yet if getting beat up was what it took to get such a stupendous raise, he thought, so be it. But a fuming Paycik simply stomped away when told he'd been supplanted. And within days, there was a new top dog running the show at Atco Trailer.

As a manager, Hale proved to be something of a wunderkind in the rough-and-tumble world of trucking. He wanted to know everything about the business, sensing he might one day strike out on his own. When real estate magnate Harry Weinberg and his brother, Nathan, stopped by to collect rent, Hale would endlessly pick their brains about the worth of nearby properties and what constituted favorable leasing terms for a truck terminal.

He hustled business by getting a list of members of the Maryland Motor Truck Association and calling each one to see if they wanted to rent a trailer.

"He was a hip-shooter in those days, a Mississippi gambler," said Bob Meehan, an executive with the White Motor Corp., a Cleveland outfit that sold the young Atco lot manager five trucks. "He was demanding, a tough buyer."

Tranchitella became a father figure to Hale, whose responsibilities with the company quickly grew. Soon the older man would task Hale with opening new offices for the company in Richmond, Va., Allentown, Pa., and Philadelphia.

"I knew I could trust him. He was a go-getter and reliable," said Tranchitella.

In fact, he grew so fond of the clever, conscientious Hale that he would tell people: "Ed is like the son I never had."

At the same time, Hale's relationship with his own father was becoming increasingly tempestuous.

When the younger Hale was first hired at Atco and informed his dad that he'd be making $125 a week at the new job, his father had snorted: "I'd rather see you be a goddamn garbage man. I can get you a job at C&P Telephone or at the gas and electric company."

Then a few months after Hale got his promotion and raise from Tranchitella, there was another deflating encounter with his dad.

This one occurred right after Ed paid cash for a brand new Oldsmobile 442. It was the ultimate "muscle car," a dazzling speed machine built, as the numbers in its name signaled, with a four-barrel carburetor, four-speed manual transmission and dual exhausts.

"It was hot!" Hale recalls. "It was a convertible, a dark brown metallic color with tan stripes and a tan interior. It was beautiful. I mean, it was *smoking!*"

Bursting with pride over his new ride, he drove it to his parents' house to show it off. But he left feeling disheartened when his father simply gazed at the car from the living room window and said: "Huh. Next time you want to go out to dinner or go to the movies, just take that car for a ride around the block."

Meaning: boy, what a dumb purchase. And it's going to suck all the money out of your pockets, too.

As the months went on, relations would become strained with another close family member, too.

At the time, business was booming at Atco. And Hale was held in such high esteem as a manager that he was able to hire his brother to run a new lot the company was opening in northeast Philadelphia. Barry Hale was 21 and he and his wife, Jean, were newlyweds when he took over the new branch with 20 trailers and very little business.

"You got one and a half phone calls a day," Barry Hale recalled. "It was like 'HELLO?'" Followed by the chirping of crickets echoing through the emptiness.

Nevertheless, Barry was happy to have the job. But when he and Jean returned to Baltimore for Thanksgiving and the Hale clan was sitting down to dinner at the Sparrow's Point house, Ed asked Barry a seemingly innocent question: "Are you going home tonight?"

"What do you mean, am I going home?" Barry replied.

He had planned to spend a couple of days relaxing in his hometown after the holiday.

"We're open tomorrow," Ed replied evenly.

Meaning: if we're open here, you better be open in Philly, too.

Barry Hale was astonished.

"It's the Friday after Thanksgiving!" he recalls of that conversation. "There's zero activity! *Nothing's* gonna happen! So I got a dose of Big Ed right out of the gate. He wasn't kidding around."

Nevertheless, at 8 a.m. the Friday after Thanksgiving, Barry's Atco lot was open for business—or no business, as it happened.

Barry would end up working for the company for two more years. But when he asked Ed for a $10 raise and was refused, he remembers thinking: "I don't think I'm going to do too well with this arrangement. There's only room for one bull moose in the forest."

Soon, he left to start his own trailer rental company. Barry Hale proved to be a savvy businessman, too. Today he owns Hale Trailer Brake and Wheel, a $150 million company based in Voorhees, N.J.

But the brothers' relationship would be strained going forward. While Barry thought Ed was too much of a hard-ass and self-promoter, Ed felt Barry was wildly judgmental and ungrateful for all the help his older brother had given him to get a toe-hold in the business.

In 1975, Tranchitella sold Atco to Industrial Bank and Trust of Philadelphia. He made provisions for Hale, now the vice-president and general manager, to stay on. By now the young man was making between $40,000-$50,000 a year when most of his friends were lucky to be making half that.

But the ever-restless Hale was already looking around for his next business opportunity, and a way to move up in the world and make even more money.

He wouldn't have to look far.

The trucking business was experiencing a gold rush of sorts. And Ed Hale was bold enough to stake a big claim.

# CHAPTER 4

## You snooze, you lose

After a client in New York agreed to rent trailers from Atco but complained about not having anyone to haul containers between the train station in Baltimore and the Pier 10 docks in Canton, a light bulb went off in Hale's head, just like in the cartoons.

"Hell," he thought, "*I* can do that."

So it was that in March of that year, he started his own trucking company, Port East Transfer Inc. It was, to put it kindly, a bare-bones operation.

"We had no trucks, no trailers, no terminals," Hale recalled.

Instead, he hired independent truckers and ran things out of the trunk of his car at first, then from his Pikesville home.

"I'd run out and stop a truck that was bobtailing," he said, referring to a tractor without the trailer, "and I'd say 'You want to make 20 bucks real quick?' And they'd go pick up a load. It was like the Wild West!"

Hale was still working for Atco and didn't hide the fact that he had started his own small trucking firm on the side. But his Atco bosses wondered if he was devoting enough time to their company. When a new supervisor asked him to choose between Atco and his fledgling business, the choice was an easy one for the kid from eastern Baltimore County who had always harbored outsized expectations of life.

He was already making more money from Port East than he was from Atco, anyway. At 28, Ed Hale was finally ready to strike out on his own.

Before long, he was running his new trucking operation in another garden spot—a cramped office trailer on Newkirk Street in Canton, this one without indoor plumbing or water.

In the winter, when he'd go to the outhouse to relieve himself and a truck would rumble overhead on Interstate 895, it would spray ice and slush that sounded like thunder as it pounded the metal roof.

Hale learned quickly that the trucking business was not for the faint of heart. Not long after starting Port East, he received a call from the traffic manager of one of his accounts, Lever Brothers. The company was preparing for a strike at its big soap factory on Holabird Avenue.

Would Hale be willing to cross the picket line? If he did, the manager promised, the company would give him all the business he could handle, which would be considerable. Lever Brothers was still one of the biggest producers of laundry products in the world, with over 1,000 employees at the Holabird plant.

Hale knew what awaited him if he defied the strikers. The threat of violence was very real. He called Ty Pruitt, one of his competitors in the business. The conversation was short and sweet.

"Are you going to cross the picket line?" Hale asked.

"I will if you will," the flinty Pruitt responded.

"OK, I will," Hale said.

He felt he had little choice.

"My drivers would have probably taken their trucks and gone someplace else to work, and I would have lost all my manpower," he explained years later. "And there was the promise—the expectation—

of more business."

A few days later, some 20 trucks in all crossed the picket line, with Ed Hale and Ty Pruitt leading the convoy. The atmosphere was charged as they rolled up. The police were maintaining a tense presence from a distance. But angry, placard-carrying men and women quickly converged on the trucks.

"There were people throwing things at us, rocks and bolts, people swearing, jumping in front of the trucks," Hale recalled.

"Oh, it was brutal," Pruitt added. "*Brutal!* The entrance to Lever Brothers was (narrow), so you really had to almost push your way through with the truck. One of my drivers, they actually spit in his face. He got out and grabbed the guy by the neck and had him locked up."

Retaliation for failing to honor the picket line was swift—and not totally unexpected by either man.

When Hale arrived early the next morning to open his facility, it looked like a war zone—literally. Someone had shot up the place and done massive damage to 10 tractors and 20 trailers.

"I don't know if they used a machine gun or what," Hale said. "Every single window was shot out and every single tire was flattened."

Ty Pruitt's trucks were also vandalized: someone had taken a tire iron and punctured every one of the radiators on his trucks.

"It was a message" from the strikers, said Pruitt. But he, like Hale, looked at it as the cost of doing business. "At the time I was young and didn't give a shit. Economically it hurt, for sure. Probably cost me a thousand dollars a truck."

The police made it clear they couldn't help. Shocking absolutely no one, the cops had been unable to find eyewitnesses to the destruction and had few clues to work with. Lever Brothers reimbursed Hale 100 per cent for the damages, but never gave him any business after that—a betrayal he never forgot.

"That was an eye-opener," he said. "It left a lasting impression on me."

It was Hale's first real trouble with unions, and it would go on to influence his feelings about organized labor for the rest of his life. He had nothing against unions before the Lever Brothers fiasco. After all, he'd been a member in good-standing of the steelworkers' and ironworkers' unions as a youth.

But why couldn't the unions recognize that, as the owner of a trucking firm now, he needed to keep his people working, too?

A few months later, Hale was driving with Sheila along Boston Street in Canton when he spotted a piece of waterfront property littered with junk piles and coal ash. A sign stuck in the ground said: "For Sale. Penn Central Railroad."

Intrigued, he stopped to investigate. Other signs saying "Keep Out" dotted the land, but Hale ignored them. As it happened, he was looking to expand his business and needed more space, and he wondered if the Penn Central lot was suitable.

In the mid-70's, Canton was a forlorn-looking neighborhood of abandoned warehouses, decrepit buildings and rotting wharves, and this place was hardly idyllic. But clambering over railroad ties, he spotted the flag at Fort McHenry in the distance and a shimmering expanse of blue water that sold him on the land immediately.

He had always been drawn to the Chesapeake Bay and he found this scene captivating.

"I thought, if you're going to build a truck terminal, why not have a nice view?" Hale recalled. "It doesn't have to be this grimy place with a cinderblock building and weeds all around it."

He took out a small business loan and bought the property for $170,000, splitting the money with the city to settle an old tax lien. He stuck an office trailer on it, cleaned it up and opened up the view. It soon caught the eye of Baltimore's energetic, irascible mayor, William Donald Schaefer.

Schaefer was on a mission to claim waterfront property for the city as part of a grand plan to develop a "Gold Coast" in Canton, envisioning a promenade that would go all the way around to Fort McHenry. He dispatched his young assistant, Mark Wasserman, to see if Hale would sell his land.

"My... recollection," Wasserman says now, "is he wanted no parts of selling it."

Hale was still new in the business and had nowhere else to park his trucks. But Schaefer refused to take no for an answer.

Soon Wasserman was back, summoning Hale to a meeting with the mayor. When he was ushered into a ceremonial room at City Hall, Hale found Schaefer striking a regal pose in an ornate chair that looked like a throne.

"I understand you're playing hardball with that property, son," Schaefer began, skipping any preliminaries.

"Well, Your Majesty," Hale shot back, "I don't have any other place to go with my business."

"I think I was going to call him 'Your Honor' and I just got flummoxed," Hale would say of the "Your Majesty" crack. "But he *did l*ook like he was on a throne."

Despite the impudent remark, the two men took an immediate liking to one another. Schaefer had a warm spot for military veterans and admired Hale's moxie. Hale appreciated the mayor's direct manner and his evident passion for Baltimore.

By the time the meeting broke up, Hale was willing to strike a verbal deal of sorts.

"I'm going to make something of myself," he told Schaefer. "Once I do and I find another place for my business, I'll sell the land to you."

The two men shook hands. Within two years, with his business growing, Hale found an 18-acre piece of property on 68th Street in Rosedale suitable for his needs.

Keeping his vow to the mayor, he sold the land on Boston Street to the city. The price: $2.3 million, a handsome return on his original

$170,000 investment. (Years later the stretch of land would become the Korean War Memorial Park and a vital piece of the waterfront promenade the hard-charging mayor had dreamed of for so long.)

Not yet 30 years old, Ed Hale was a certified millionaire. But instead of celebrating, he decided to plow nearly every penny of his settlement check back into his business. By now it had grown to include 50 trucks, both company-owned and owner-operated.

"He called us into the office the next day," recalled Ken Jones, then a newly-hired Port East employee. "He told us how much he got for the land. Then he told us he could retire and live comfortably for the rest of his life. But he said that wasn't what he wanted to do. He was going to invest this money back into the company.

"He wanted us to know that he wanted the company to grow, and that we were all going to keep our jobs. It got us incredibly energized."

For Hale, though, the rapid growth of his trucking firm did not come without headaches. His operation soon became a target for local 557 of the Teamsters union, which pressed to organize his drivers, roughly 40 in number.

Hale wanted no part of the union. His stance on unions had hardened since becoming embroiled in the Lever Brothers strike. By now he had seen the Teamsters run other companies into the ground. He found the Teamster work rules abhorrent, along with the dictum that management wasn't allowed to communicate directly with workers, and had to instead go through shop stewards.

He wondered: why was the union attempting to bully its way into a heretofore content work force? What was the point of that? To cause trouble for trouble's sake?

"I thought: not only am I a fair guy, I'm a good guy, a working guy," he said. "I'm just like you. Why are you *doing* this to me?"

To anyone who'd listen, he'd insist: "The union doesn't give a rat's ass about the rank-and-file." And he'd tell his workers, only half-jokingly: "If you fucking guys organize me, I'll make this place a banana stand."

Nevertheless, he had no choice but to schedule an election to determine whether his drivers wanted a union shop. A booth was set up at his truck terminal for secret balloting. On hand to oversee the process was one of Hale's people, as well as a Teamster representative and an official from the National Labor Relations Board.

When the balloting was complete, the NLRB agent announced the results: 39-0 against union representation, with one ballot defaced.

Amid cheers from Hale's drivers, the agent asked: "Want me to read what it says on the defaced ballot?"

Hale shrugged. "Sure, go ahead."

The agent took a deep breath. "It says, 'Fuck you, unions. Unions suck. Unions out."

Now the cheers and whooping were deafening.

To celebrate the resounding victory—and to stick it to the Teamsters one more time— Hale treated everyone to drinks and dinner at Jimmy's Seafood Restaurant on Holabird Avenue, a well-known union hangout.

"Everyone was so relieved," he recalled of that night. "There had been such tension. The Teamsters never tried to organize me in Baltimore again."

Not only that, but he would go on to beat back union challenges to his facilities in Pittsburgh, Boston and Philadelphia as his trucking empire grew.

Still, as all-consuming as his new business was, the young mogul remained restless. Already he was looking around for other opportunities to make a name for himself.

And once again, in an almost spiritual fashion, he'd be drawn to the water.

# CHAPTER 5
## The Midas Touch Redux

Before the Boston Street facility was sold to the city, it would prove to have an enormous impact on Ed Hale's fortunes in a totally unexpected way.

The reason: it had a pier that he rented to a barge line. And in addition to enjoying the spectacular view of Fort McHenry, the famous star-shaped fort that defended Baltimore Harbor from the British in the War of 1812, Hale began studying how the Norfolk, Baltimore and Carolina Barge Line operated.

He soon arrived at a predictable conclusion: he could do the job better.

Containerization was in the midst of transforming the trucking, shipping and railroad industries. With standardized dimensions, steel containers carrying virtually everything could be loaded, unloaded and stacked efficiently for transport by any mode without being opened.

Hale had noticed that the NB&C barges had space for 60 containers. What if he bought his own barges and outfitted them to carry even *more* containers? Wouldn't that save on truck fuel costs and be a more efficient way to transport cargo up and down the East Coast?

Wouldn't it also be a boon to the environment? After all, more containers on barges meant fewer exhaust-spewing trucks hauling the same cargo on the roads.

Hale had actually approached NB&C about buying the company earlier and found the owner to be agreeable. But when his father condescendingly told him to "stop messing around and buy those barges," a defiant Hale promptly called the owner, Leigh Hogshire, and called off the deal.

That did it, Hale thought. Now I'm *definitely* buying my own barges.

First stop was Houma, Louisiana, where he discovered two barges for sale in a swampy lowland. They were, at first glance, a soggy, sorry-looking sight.

"The barges were submerged," Hale recalled. "They would sink them in the bayou so hurricanes wouldn't come in and float them away."

Hale sent a tugboat down to Houma and had the barges towed back to Baltimore. They were named the Norfolk Trader and the Philadelphia Trader. Retrofitted and loaded a certain way, they could accommodate a whopping 420 containers. And in 1985, Hale Container Lines officially opened for business at 1801 South Clinton Street in Canton.

To the delight of such champions of East Baltimore as Sen. Barbara Mikulski (D-Md) and Rep. Helen Delich Bentley (R-Md), Hale had two more barges, the Baltimore Trader and Boston Trader, built at Bethlehem Steel's Sparrow's Point shipyard.

Even though the barges would cost him between $600,000 and $800,000 more than they would if built elsewhere, Hale said he contracted with Beth Steel "out of a sense of loyalty." The kid who had once made $4 an hour working in the steel mill had never forgotten how good the mill was to the thousands of young people hired to decent-paying jobs right out of high school.

(Thinking it would look far too pretentious, though, Hale refused to christen his barges with champagne. "Fuck no!" he laughed when that was suggested. "It's a *barge*."

(Instead, when Bentley, now a former congresswoman, was invited to help launch one of his first vessels, she christened it with—what else?—a bottle of National Bohemian beer, Baltimore's beloved "Natty Boh.")

At its height, Hale's fleet would consist of seven barges—one, the Liberty Trader, would be bigger than a football field and capable of hauling 730 containers. It would also include four tugboats: the Ashley Hale and Alexandra Hale, named for the two daughters he fathered later with his girlfriend, Michele Guttierrez; the Carol Hale, named for his mother; and the Larkin Hale, chosen in honor of his grandmother, whose maiden name was Larkin.

For the next dozen years, Hale would have barges running up and down the East Coast, as well as to such far-flung destinations as Alexandria, Egypt, French Guiana, the Canadian Maritime province of New Brunswick, and Crete, the largest of the Greek islands.

He would soon be the Port of Baltimore's biggest employer and serve as an advisor to Mayor Schaefer on port issues in addition to accompanying the mayor on trade missions overseas.

In his own unique way, Hale even managed to forge tiny diplomatic breakthroughs that would help his hometown. He chartered tugs and barges with Orient Overseas Container Line, a huge shipping firm headquartered in Hong Kong. And his influence with Captain Shiuan Y. Kuo, chairman of Evergreen Shipping in Taipei, helped promote trade between Taiwan and Baltimore.

(On a summer trip to sweltering Taipei with Schaefer, the Taiwanese were also treated to the surreal sight of Schaefer and Hale, exhausted from jet-lag, singing an absolutely horrid karaoke version of "Jingle Bell Rock."

(Both men had taken the stage thinking the song machine was

programmed for "Jingle Bells." And since neither knew the words to "Jingle Bell Rock," they were promptly booed off the stage in a country where karaoke was considered only slightly less important than life, death and baseball.)

When Saudi Arabian Prince Salman bin Sultan visited Baltimore in the late 80's, Schaefer asked Hale to give the prince a tour of the port. Hale hosted the Saudi delegation aboard his luxury yacht, the 85-foot-long Exuberance, which had once been the America's Cup Committee boat.

Hale was told that Prince Salman, the governor of Riyadh, the Saudi capital, spoke no English. But at one point, as the two men sat alone in the back of the yacht, the prince tapped Hale's leg and whispered: "I bet you have a lot of fun on this boat."

Incredulous, Hale said: "You speak English!"

"I do have my moments," the prince replied with an impish grin.

"It was just like in 'One Flew Over the Cuckoo's Nest,'" Hale would recall, "when Jack Nicholson is sitting next to the Chief and the Chief has been silent the whole movie—and suddenly he speaks for the first time. And Nicholson looks at him and says: 'Goddamn, Chief! You can *talk!*'"

In the next breath, the prince mentioned that he, too, had a yacht, a monster 167-footer at his beck and call.

"Well, you win then," Hale said with a laugh.

"But I can't have as much fun on it," the prince said wistfully, "because my wife is around all the time."

The two men hit it off so well that Hale was promptly invited to Riyadh with a select delegation of American businessmen, which helped him cultivate ties with the National Shipping Company of Saudi Arabia.

In addition to his burgeoning barge business, Hale's trucking business was booming, too. He was now operating 500 trucks and countless trailers from 13 terminals all over the East Coast and extending out to Cincinnati, Ohio.

Yet no matter how successful he became, he could never escape the sense that he was constantly being judged as someone from "the other side of the tracks."

Around this time, he was invited by a tennis-playing acquaintance to a swanky dinner party in the Greenspring Valley. But the conversation around the table soon took an ugly turn—at least for Hale—when the well-heeled guests started sniping at people from Dundalk.

"They were ridiculing everything about us!" he recalled. "How we looked, how we talked, how we dressed!"

Hale seethed, but said nothing. Still, the bad-mouthing of his home turf stunned him. Until that moment, he had never thought of himself as having grown up in a hard-scrabble setting, never mind a place that would possibly be the target of derision.

Now, even with his trucking and barge firms generating between $75 million and $100 million, he was sure the "blue-bloods" still thought of him as an ignorant redneck who had somehow lucked out in business.

At times, he wondered if his father felt the same way. Only what happened at these times was far more hurtful.

One day, not long after Hale had begun using a computer for his business for the first time, his father visited his office.

"Look at this thing!" Hale said, pointing with pride to the shiny new terminal. "It's doing my payroll, accounts payable, accounts receivable, balance sheets, everything!"

But instead of marveling at this new technology and perhaps praising his son for being resourceful in acquiring it, the elder Hale shook his head and muttered: "They're trying to computerize our warehouse. Computers are ruining everything."

A short while later, as soon as Hale saw the tail-lights of his father's car leaving, he got on the phone to Joe Poiter, the man who had sold him the machine.

"When the new computers come out," he said, fairly spitting out the words," put me on the top of the list to buy one."

# CHAPTER 6

## No Business for the Weak

Within six months of buying his tugboats, Hale had another familiar problem to deal with: more union pressure.

When one of his tugboats docked in lower Manhattan, a couple of henchmen of Alfonso Cornette, the head of local 333 of the International Longshoreman's Association, swaggered aboard.

They doled out a case of beer to the crew and promptly announced: "You guys are getting fucked by this guy Hale."

Cornette's men promised the crew more money, better working conditions—everything but the moon and the stars—if it joined the ILA. At the time, the New York docks were heavily infiltrated by elements of organized crime. Hale would soon be told by James Kallstrom, former head of the FBI's New York office, that Cornette was mobbed-up, too.

"He's not a 'made guy,'" Hale was told by Kallstrom, who would go on to direct the bureau's investigation of the mysterious explosion of TWA flight 800 off the coast of Long Island in July of 1996. "But he's probably some low-level (associate.) These guys are tough guys. They play hardball."

Hale took the news calmly, even stoically.

"I was impressed with Ed—just the way he carried himself and how he spoke," Kallstrom says now. "... His reaction was: 'I'm not gonna let these guys run me out of the business.'"

Nevertheless, Hale was again forced to hold a union election. His workers could vote to continue the status quo or join either the ILA or the Seafarers International Union.

The final tally was a foregone conclusion, especially with the tacit threat of mob violence in the air. (One worker later told Hale that he'd had a gun held to his head and been told in no uncertain terms which way to vote.)

The ILA won handily. And the result was a categorical disaster for Hale's barge business.

After its victory, the union's first order of business was to replace all of Hale's tugboat workers—some 50 in all—with crewmen who had more ILA seniority.

"They were total useless goons," Hale recalled. "At the end of the shift, someone would be rolling around on the dock, holding his leg, faking injury."

As he had feared, workers' compensation claims soared, the volume of work slowed and Hale was forced to deal with one headache after another caused by malingering crewmen.

He reacted with typical Ed Hale stubbornness: each time a tug developed any sort of problem that the crews complained about—even something as minor as a clogged toilet—he'd take the boat out of commission. Then he'd charter a boat with a non-union crew to pull his barges.

Within two years, tiring of all the union problems, he had sold his tugs and was out of the business for good.

Nevertheless, his continuing anti-union stance earned Hale a good deal of enmity in Baltimore, even as his barge business flourished. The longshoremen grumbled about him incessantly. Richie Hughes, the head of the ILA, called him "Schaefer's Rasputin" and accused him of giving the mayor bad advice on the port.

Most unsettling of all, Hale started receiving death threats. Defiant as ever, he would walk around the Clinton Street offices with a baseball cap on which he'd painted a bulls-eye target. "He would scare the hell out of us with that," Ken Jones remembered.

Hale also began carrying a gun and wearing a flak jacket to public events. He hired a bodyguard. He had his car outfitted with a gizmo that could detect booby-traps in the road.

And he took other security precautions—some to humorous effect.

"Ed drove a Jaguar—all the time," recalled Harry Lipsitz, who went to work for Hale as an accountant in 1983. "There was one of these union confrontations with the maritime people. So one day I come in the office. And I'm driving the Taurus, a company car. And Ed says 'Harry, I'd like to give you my car for the company car and get rid of the Taurus. I'm going to get a new Lincoln Town Car.'"

Here Lipsitz smiled merrily.

"And I may have figured it out," he continued, "or a secretary told me: Ed was afraid everyone knew what kind of car he was driving and that he was a target. And they wouldn't figure a cool guy like Ed would be driving a blue Lincoln Town Car and his accountant would be driving this really snazzy Jaguar."

But Hale soon gained a reputation for playing hardball, too, as his barge business thrived. When a shipping company called Topgallant owed him $320,000 and was slow to pay up, he took matters into his own hands.

After Topgallant cargo was loaded onto one of his barges in New York and the vessel had begun its trip to Boston, Hale ordered the tugboat captain to drop anchor away from the shipping lanes near Brooklyn's Verrazano Bridge.

He then instructed Lipsitz to call Topgallant and deliver a simple message: they would get their cargo when he got his money.

"Ed said: 'Until the money is wired, we're keeping the cargo on the barge,'" Lipsitz said.

Predictably, the Topgallant people went nuts. Cursing and screaming, they protested that what Hale was doing was against the law. They also threatened legal action.

"I felt pressure to give in," Lipsitz recalled. "But Ed said: 'Show me the money.'"

As the tense standoff continued and the calls from the Topgallant people grew more heated, Hale himself took over the negotiations.

"I told them: 'You can threaten me and it doesn't mean shit to me,'" he recalled. "'I want my money. No cash, no splash.'"

Not until later that night, when Hale received confirmation that the cash had been wired, did the barge weigh anchor and start for Boston again.

Closer to home, another incident solidified his reputation as a young businessman who would not be intimidated—and who wouldn't let his workers get pushed around, either

Returning from lunch to his 68th Street office one day, Hale found his secretary, Marie Hamburg, crying at her desk. She said the manager of GMC Trucks next door, a man named George Joseph, had just called.

In a harsh, angry tone, Joseph had demanded that Hale remove three containers that Joseph said were on his property, containers adorned with a sign that advised motorists on nearby Pulaski Highway: "Port East Transfer - Turn Left at Next Light."

Now it was Hale who went thermonuclear.

He promptly called Joseph back. "Now you have a man on the phone," he said. "You got something to tell me?"

When Jones reiterated that the containers had to be moved, Hale said he'd comply. But in the next breath, he told Joseph that a recent survey indicated the fence for GMC Trucks was encroaching on his property, over an area 200 feet by 40 feet.

"You have until Friday to take it off," Hale said.

Then he hung up.

Hale had the offending containers removed from the truck store property minutes later. But the next day, a telegram from GMC's headquarters' in Pontiac, MI. arrived at Hale's office, warning him that the company would file charges if he destroyed its fence.

Nevertheless, when the fence wasn't removed by 4 p.m. the following Friday, passers-by were treated to the surreal sight of Hale and several workers, including Ken Jones, descending on the fence with forklifts and acetylene torches.

Joseph and some of his staff looked on in astonishment.

"You're crazy!" Joseph sputtered. "You can' do that!"

"Cut the fence," Hale told his workers.

Within seconds, sparks from the acetylene torches filled the air, starting tiny fires in the underbrush. Not long after, the fence came down with a loud *WHOMP!*

Joseph immediately called the police. But when the cops arrived and Hale showed them his site plan with the property boundaries, they declined to arrest the Port East owner. Instead, they told Joseph to consider pursuing a civil action against Hale.

"Ed wasn't being a cowboy," Ken Jones recalled. "He won't allow people to disrespect his people."

From then on, Hale, says: "People knew you didn't trifle with me." He laughs. "After that, people were even saying: 'That Hale, he knows *karate!*'"

But by the 90's, Hale's barge business would begin to go south, driven, in large part, by a man named Umberto "Bert" Guido.

Guido, from Brooklyn, N.Y. started a barge company called Columbia Coastal Transport and was soon under-cutting Hale's business. Columbia Coastal was quoting lower prices everywhere. Within two years, it was operating in Baltimore and gobbling up Hale's routes.

Another call from Hale to Kallstrom confirmed that Guido was a low-level associate of the Genovese crime family, probably involved in mob-run "sweetheart deals" on the New York docks.

"You couldn't be in that type of business without being associated with organized crime," Kallstrom says now from his Connecticut home.

Hale liked Guido personally, but recognized he was dealing with a dangerous individual. Nevertheless, he filed suit in federal court in Baltimore, claiming that Guido was violating anti-trust rules and trying to drive him out of business.

"That was the Ed Hale hubris!" said Kevin O'Connor, a long-time friend who was then the head of the Baltimore County Firefighter's Union. "It was: 'I'm Ed Hale, and I'm standing toe-to-toe with anyone, including the Genovese Family.'"

At the height of the tension between the two barge magnates, Hale, along with his two young daughters and a woman named Suzie Walters, was involved in a frightening plane crash.

His Cessna 206 had just taken off from his farm in Easton, Md., bound for Baltimore, when engine parts flew out of the cowling and the propeller died. With the kids screaming, the pilot was forced to ditch in the frigid waters of the Chesapeake Bay.

No one was hurt, but Hale's sense of vulnerability was ramped up. So was his paranoia. He wondered: could Bert Guido possibly be behind the crash?

"I thought maybe someone had gotten into the hangar and done something to the plane," Hale said.

He again called Kallstrom, who urged him to have the engine tested at an independent lab. No evidence of tampering was found. But years of dealing with tough, ruthless adversaries in the cutthroat trucking and shipping industries had convinced Hale that he couldn't be too careful.

The legal battle between Hale and Guido came to a head when

the two sides agreed to a mediation session, presided over by Judge Susan K. Guavey, at the federal courthouse in Baltimore. After a long, draining day, Hale eventually agreed to sell his barge business to Columbia Coastal for $9.7 million.

After the deal was struck, Hale and Guido shook hands in the bright sunshine outside the federal courthouse. In a celebratory mood, Guido smiled and said: "Hey, let's go over to Little Italy and have some dinner."

But Hale was in no mood for drinks and chit-chat with his old adversary.

"Give me a couple of days, Bert," he said. "I thought you were gonna whack me."

Whether the Columbia Coastal owner ended up having a nice Italian meal and a bottle of wine in Baltimore later that evening isn't known.

But it was of no interest to Ed Hale, who was done with his former rival and relieved to be rid of a business that had caused him more than a few headaches.

Besides, just a short while earlier, he had faced someone far scarier than Bert Guido.

Namely, a divorce court judge.

# CHAPTER 7
## Trouble in Shangri-la

In 1979, Sheila Hale found her dream home on a gentle hill in Timonium, Md., with a sweeping view of Loch Raven Reservoir and the Dulaney Valley that seemed to go on forever.

Pot Spring House was a magnificent historic mansion, thought to have been built in the late 1700's or early 1800's. It had 16 bedrooms, 4.5 bathrooms, six working fireplaces, a 40-foot-long entrance hall dominated by an enormous wedding cake chandelier, two-foot-thick stone walls and formal gardens.

Wallace Warfield, the American socialite who became the Duchess of Windsor after her infamous affair with Edward VIII led him to abdicate the throne of England, had summered there in the early part of the 20th century.

Sheila Hale fell in love with the house—which was selling for $225,000—the moment she saw it.

"I... got right on the phone after 10 minutes and said 'Ed, get over here. And bring a check,'" she recalled.

Her husband was not quite as enamored of the place. But with his businesses prospering and the family outgrowing the house in Pikesville, near Woodholme Country Club, Ed Hale was intrigued with the possibilities. He had always loved a good fixer-upper. And he was willing to placate his wife, too.

"She wanted to live like a fairy princess," he would say later.

But Sheila insisted she had only practical reasons for wanting to move to the imposing white stone house. One was the need to relocate to a neighborhood with good schools and plenty of kids for 13-year-old Eddie Jr. to play with.

"We (also) needed room to entertain, because we were entertaining a lot," she said. "We had a fundraiser for Walter Mondale there. We'd have customers, all our employees from New Jersey and Virginia, and Baltimore people. We would have 150 people there ... and (some) would spend the night. Because there was a lot of drinking going on and you don't want to turn these people loose in the night."

Sheila Hale was also a self-described "history nut" intent on saving the aging manse from further decay. She also confessed to "a Norman Rockwell vision" of everyone in the extended Hale family, from babies to old people, gathering at the house for holidays such as Thanksgiving and Christmas.

The Hales undertook a complete restoration of the mansion, from the roof to the basement, which included replacing old hardware, electrical wiring and plumbing, as well as re-plastering walls and sanding floors. Also refurbished were the exquisite chandelier, originally hung in 1936 and believed to be made from Waterford crystal, and the quaint six-room cottage behind the house.

As the remodeling progressed, however, Ed Hale began grumbling that the house was "a money pit." This was underscored when a ceiling between the second and third floors collapsed, sending some 20 terrified raccoons and equally-frightened workers bolting for the nearest windows.

"Uh, we have a problem," one of the contractors told Hale that day.

Hearing of this raccoon Woodstock in the rafters, Hale now

envisioned great gobs of his hard-earned money being sucked non-stop into the house for pest control and a myriad of other things.

Nevertheless, the raccoons were evicted and the restoration proceeded. Final cost of the project: a cool $250,000. After that, Sheila launched into the decorating phase with a passion. She studied books about old Colonial homes and traveled frequently to Colonial Williamsburg in Virginia to get ideas for using authentic Colonial colors and period furnishings.

But when the beautiful house was spruced up and sparkling like a jewel, and the fancy parties began in earnest, Ed Hale was anything but thrilled.

"I kept asking myself: 'What am I doing here? Is that all there is?'" he recalled. "Now I was subjected to the blue-bloods and I was bored by it. They have joyless lives."

Hale was becoming unhappy in his marriage, too. Sheila could sense it. They had separated briefly in 1975, and now life with Ed, she felt, was "like walking on eggshells. He was angry all the time and always complaining, about the house, his business, you name it. He was out playing tennis all the time."

But for Ed Hale, the problems ran even deeper than Sheila could imagine, all the way back to a nervous 19-year-old about to enter the service and feeling pressured to tie the knot, because that's what you did back then if you were a stand-up guy and knocked up your girlfriend.

"I was never really happy in the marriage," he explained years later. "It was a joyless, loveless, no-affection relationship that we had. There were times when the idea of going home turned me off so badly that I would make an excuse to go someplace.

"I would play tennis seven days a week just to stay away from her. I didn't want to be there. I was looking to get out of the marriage."

Close friends and family members could sense Ed and Sheila growing apart. But for the most part, the couple managed to hide their discontent from the rest of the world.

"On the surface," Sheila said, "it looked like a totally normal marriage. We had our social life, we had all our friends, and it was fine. I don't think he knew we were headed for this big blow-up."

One day in the spring of 1983, Eddie Jr. stopped at the mailbox and discovered an odd-looking envelope addressed to Sheila. He ripped it open and began reading the note inside, which was composed of letters of all shapes and sizes cut from newspapers and magazines and pasted on a sheet of paper.

But the boy soon gave up trying to decipher it and brought it to Sheila.

"Mommy, what *is* this?" he asked.

At first Sheila was just as bewildered.

"It was one of those (letters) that looked like a ransom note," Sheila recalled. "It just said: 'Ed (is) messing around and you need to get your head up and pay attention.' It was just so bizarre. I didn't know whether to take it seriously. Is this a hoax? Is someone trying to drive a wedge between me and my husband?"

When Ed came home, Sheila showed him the letter. Ed went into a towering rage. Crimson-faced, with the veins in his neck popping out, he denied any wrong-doing. And he vowed to hunt down and punish the whacko that had sent such an upsetting letter to his wife.

"I'm going to get to the bottom of this!" he roared to Sheila. "I'm calling the FBI!"

But by this point, Sheila was on high alert for any sign that her husband was straying.

A few weeks earlier, Ed had announced that he was heading off to Bermuda to play tennis with a friend, claiming that the friend had won an all-expenses-paid trip.

"Little red flags were going up at that point," Sheila said. "But I thought: whatever. Ed was very testy in those days. He was very wound up and grouchy."

There was also this: months earlier, Ed had thrown a company picnic and insisted that there was no reason for Sheila to attend. That same day, Sheila's brother, Milton, had spotted Ed driving around Patapsco State Park with a woman who had long, straight black hair, just like Sheila's.

Only it wasn't Sheila.

Now, with the arrival of the strange-looking letter, Sheila decided: "It was time for me to play Sherlock Holmes."

She drove to the trucking office in Rosedale and went digging through her husband's expense files. She soon found his American Express bills. Included were all sorts of bills from the Bermuda trip: hotel, restaurant, bar tabs, etc.

Each bill was for two people. And far from being a free trip, each bill had been paid by Ed.

"And that's when I knew," she said.

Her husband was having an affair.

Sheila waited in the office that day until Ed returned from an appointment and confronted him. At first, he went into the standard default mode of many cheating spouses, sputtering and stammering and denying everything.

"But he saw me sitting there with the receipts, and he knew the jig was up," she said.

Ed admitted he'd been seeing another black-haired beauty named Michele Gutierrez, the general receptionist for Port East Transfer. He also talked of wanting out of the marriage for some time.

"Then he confessed to a whole bunch of other stuff," Sheila recalled.

It was a laundry list of infidelities that left her slack-jawed. But Ed Hale saw his affairs as the inevitable result of a relationship on the rocks, one that had foundered for years and left him feeling forlorn and vulnerable.

There was also another issue causing a growing rift between

them: Ed wanted to have more children and Sheila didn't. He didn't think it was healthy for Eddie Jr. to grow up without brothers or sisters. But Ed says when he expressed his desire to have another child, Sheila snapped: "*You* have it."

"Was I an angel? No way," Ed said later. "I worked harder than anyone I know. But at the same time, I was very lonely. I was married at 19 and faithful to her up to the age of 28. When I say faithful, the only woman I ever had sex with was her."

A few weeks later, the two drove to Loch Raven Reservoir to try to hash things out. Ed made it clear he wanted a divorce. But Sheila didn't. She had other, more conflicted feelings, which she attempted to explain to her husband.

"I thought: 'Ok, you've been stupid,'" she recalled thinking of Ed's behavior. "But my whole thing was family, keeping the family intact. I firmly believe in that. And despite many hard times in the marriage, I (had) always stuck it out. Married is married, and that's the end of that song."

Nevertheless, from that point on, the marriage unraveled quickly. The couple soon separated. Ed moved out of the mansion into a one-bedroom apartment in Parkville.

"It was one of the happiest days of my life," he says now. He had the family attorney, Henry Belsky, draw up a separation agreement for Sheila to sign.

"Ed says to me: 'I'm going to take care of you and Eddie,'" she recalled. "'I'll pay all the bills. You'll still live in the house. Everything will go on as normal, no interruptions, blah, blah, blah."

Sheila was scheduled to go to the Chelsea Flower Show in London at the end of May with her sister and the local garden club. It was a trip that had been booked months in advance. Harried and preoccupied as she prepared to depart, she said she signed the document Belsky had prepared without studying it.

"I was still upset and I didn't want to get a divorce," she said. ". . .

And Henry said everything would be explained to me later."

Ed says he urged Sheila to hire an attorney of her own, but that Sheila insisted on having Belsky represent her, too.

"She was crying and saying 'I don't *want* another attorney! I trust him!'" Ed recalled.

It was clear that Sheila Hale still held out hope for reconciliation. Then, one day that fall, Ed called the Pot Spring house with an unusual request. It was a conversation Sheila will never forget.

"It was the height of chutzpah!" she says now with a laugh. "I'm standing in the butler's pantry. That's where the phone was on the wall in those days. My parents were having their retirement home built in South Carolina, so they were living in Pot Spring with Eddie and me.

"I get this phone call and Ed says: 'I'm taking Michele to wherever it was, Mexico.' He had bought me luggage for Christmas the year before. And he wanted to know if he could borrow it for Michele."

Sheila did not take the request well, launching into a meltdown loud enough to be heard in Pennsylvania.

"I went nuts!" she recalls. "I had the phone receiver in my hand and I literally banged the (base of the phone) so hard that it came off the wall. My mother was in the kitchen and she was aghast."

So much for any chance of reconciliation.

Soon, Sheila was being told by friends and family members that she was being shafted by the separation agreement she'd signed. You need to hire a first-class lawyer of your own to protect your interests and look after your son, she was told.

A friend introduced her to Shale Stiller, a top attorney with the venerable Baltimore firm Frank, Bernstein, Conaway and Goldman. She was impressed by Stiller's calm demeanor and his empathy for the inequity she faced in the agreement.

Stiller was already a legal heavyweight with a big reputation. He'd been hired by former Maryland Gov. Harry Hughes as the lead counsel to represent the state in the Old Court Savings and Loan scandal, in which bank president Jeffrey Levitt was ultimately imprisoned for embezzlement.

With Stiller in her corner and her husband showing no signs of mending the marriage, there was no mistaking where Ed and Sheila Hale were headed now.

They were going to court.

And both knew things were about to get ugly.

# CHAPTER 8

## A Judgment for the Ages

Sheila Thacker-Hale formally filed for divorce in 1987 on the grounds of adultery and abandonment.

Her lawyers zeroed in on the separation agreement with a vengeance. They sought to have it rescinded on the grounds that it was procured through undue influence, fraud, duress and negligent representation, contending Belsky was wrong to have represented both parties in a marital dispute.

The matter wound its way through the legal system until a 1988 ruling that the separation agreement was "unconscionable," as it provided Sheila with only 4 per cent of Ed's assets, thought to have been $5 million at the time. (He maintained they were worth closer to $2 million.)

Judge James T. Smith, a former Baltimore County councilman, also ruled that Ed Hale had fraudulently "used sexual relations to make his wife believe that he was interested in reconciling," when all he wanted was to get her signature on the agreement and protect his wealth.

The divorce trial took place in Baltimore County Circuit Court in November of 1988. Due to his prior experience with the case,

Judge Smith was assigned to the non-jury proceedings.

By then, though, the stakes for Ed Hale were much higher.

For one thing, his wealth had increased dramatically. Sheila's lawyers now estimated it at $15 million, which meant he had far more to lose. The court was also likely to look askance at the fact Ed had fathered two children with Michele Gutierrez—Ashley Hale, born in 1984, and Alexandra Hale, born three years later—before the divorce proceedings had even begun.

Nevertheless, Hale was confident of a good outcome in the weeks leading up to the trial. On the advice of Henry Belsky, he had hired an aggressive, high-powered attorney of his own: Paul Mark Sandler, of the Baltimore firm Freishtat and Sandler.

"(Ed) called him a rat terrier," Sheila remembered. "He thought: I've got this guy who's going to tear her apart."

Ed Hale was also heartened by a favorable scouting report on Jim Smith that he'd received from an old friend, Dennis F. Rasmussen, a former Baltimore County Executive.

"I said (Smith) was an excellent councilman, highly-respected, a sharp guy, had a reputation of being fair" as a judge, Rasmussen recalled.

On the first day of the trial—in a preemptive move that had been discussed with Sandler beforehand—Ed Hale took the stand and promptly announced that he was an "adulterer."

"I did that," he says now, "because I was told they had 18 women on a list they were going to call as witnesses" who would testify to his infidelities with them.

(Years later, when asked if he'd had sex with all 18 women, Hale paused before replying: "No, but quite a few of them.")

As Hale's testimony unfolded, Smith was amazed at how nonchalant the trucking and shipping magnate was about his marital indiscretions.

"He made it obvious he ran around with women and had all

kinds of girlfriends," Smith recalled.

The judge's incredulity only increased when Ed admitted asking to borrow Sheila's luggage for his girlfriend's use on their vacation trip to Mexico.

"I thought: What balls! You brazen son of a bitch! I mean, *come on!*" Smith recalled.

But Smith came to admire Hale's candor and withering introspection, in particular his pronouncement to the court that he had been a terrible husband and a terrible father.

"(Then) he was asked about Sheila," Smith recalled, "and he said 'My God, she was 150 per cent the perfect wife!' I mean, you had to like the guy! He was just so *out* there. So I don't remember it as being a rancorous divorce."

Yet the two parties involved clearly disagreed with that assessment.

Sandler's aggressive and antagonistic cross-examination of Sheila on the witness stand unnerved her, particularly insinuations that she herself had fooled around in the marriage during trips to San Francisco to see her sister.

Shale Stiller would point out that Sheila had always taken Eddie Jr. on each of these trips and that she had no romantic interest in California. But Sandler's tactics got under her skin anyway.

"I'd think: OK, find your Zen moment. Be calm. Focus on Shale and try to get through this," she recalled.

At other times during the grilling, she found a measure of black humor by staring at Sandler's monogrammed shirts and the initials PMS and thinking: "Maybe *that's* your problem."

Ultimately, though, the trial took an ominous turn for Ed Hale.

First, his old lawyer, Henry Belsky, broke down sobbing on the witness stand when scolded by Judge Smith for initially representing both parties in the dispute, an egregious breach of ethics. Watching his blubbering attorney issuing a guilt-wracked mea culpa, an incredulous Hale could only think: *Are you kidding me?*

"Right at that moment," Hale says now, "Sandler looks at me and says: 'We just lost the case.' But my take on that was that Sandler was going to use it as an excuse if we lost."

Then a man named Ray Turchi, a former executive vice-president of Port East Transfer who had left the company on bad terms a year earlier, testified.

Turchi told the court that Hale had admitted to others that he'd had sex with Sheila years earlier to make her believe he was interested in reconciliation, when, in fact, he wasn't. Listening to this, Ed seethed.

"I didn't do that to make her think I wanted to reconcile," he said later. "I just felt sorry for her." Later he would call Turchi "a back-stabbing liar" and add: "It was the worst betrayal of my entire life."

But the damage was done. Belsky's breakdown was damaging enough; Turchi's testimony was a figurative dagger in Hale's side. He was now resigned to getting hammered by the judge. The only question was how hard Smith would flog him in the pocketbook.

For Sheila, though, the atmosphere in the courtroom was tense in the moments before the verdict was rendered.

She had no idea what Jim Smith, who struck her as a kindly magistrate with vast reservoirs of common sense, was thinking about the case. And from the outset she had never discussed a final settlement figure with her attorneys.

"I had no number in my head, honest to God," she would recall. Stiller, she said, "kept talking to me about trying to find all of Ed's assets. He said: 'You know you're entitled to half.'

"But we didn't know what that number was. Was it $2 million? Was it $10 million? We had no idea."

Attempting to calm herself and her legal team in the moments before the judge entered the courtroom, she took Stiller's hand and the hand of her other attorney, Peter Axelrad, and said: "Guys, whatever happens, you did the best you could. And I love you and thank you."

Ed Hale, on the other hand, sat there glowering, fuming at his lawyer and expecting the worst.

Which is exactly what he got.

When a poker-faced Judge Smith finally took the bench, he got right down to business. In a calm, measured voice, he began ticking off the terms of the settlement. The bottom line: Ed was ordered to pay Sheila the whopping sum of $6.4 million.

She would receive $120,000 in alimony for the next 20 years along with an additional $3.9 million, $550,000 of which was to be paid within the next four months.

It was the largest divorce settlement in Maryland history.

When Smith finished, the courtroom was dead silent at first, followed by audible gasps. Sheila herself was shocked—and confused.

"I couldn't wait to get out of the courtroom to talk to Shale and say: 'Really? What just *happened*?'"

She glanced over at Ed, who was now beet-red, the veins in his neck popping like whipcords again.

"I thought: my God, he's going to have a stroke!" Sheila recalled. "He's going to have apoplexy! He's going to lose it right here! Oh, it was horrifying to see. It really was."

In that moment, Sheila knew two things about her ex-husband beyond the shadow of a doubt.

"I knew Ed was madder than he'd ever been in his life," she said. "And I knew he wanted to murder Paul Mark Sandler."

The verdict, Hale would say later, left him reeling for one of the few times in his life.

"I could not believe I had lost so badly," he said. "I knew there was going to be huge financial damage to the business. And I was angry at Sheila for playing the poor widow woman."

He was also, as Sheila had correctly observed, entertaining homicidal thoughts about Paul Mark Sandler.

"I had a terrible lawyer," he would say whenever anyone expressed amazement at how hard he'd been hammered in the divorce. He quickly hired another local attorney, Bruce Hoffman, to, he says, "clean up the mess" in the trial's aftermath.

In retrospect, Smith said he could sense Ed Hale's increasing dissatisfaction with Sandler from the very beginning of the trial.

"Paul Mark was tedious," Smith recalled. "And with a client like Ed... to take a very methodical approach with a guy who's all over the board is, you know, incongruous. Paul Mark Sandler is generally a very good lawyer. And he's very expensive. With the results Ed got, he probably didn't like that, either."

News of the judgment was blared on the front page of the *Baltimore Sun* the next day, and soon had tongues wagging all over town. Friends and foes alike seemed stunned by the huge amount awarded Sheila.

"Of course, when the ruling came down," Dennis Rasmussen said years later with a laugh, "Ed called me up and said: 'I just want you to know that your 'fair judge' just shoved it up my ass."

Harry Lipsitz, Hale's accountant, recalled: "I used to say this, and Ed didn't find it funny: he did to the divorce record what Bob Beamon did to the broad jump record."

Yes, just as Beamon had shattered that record in the 1968 Mexico City Olympics, so had Hale shattered the Free State record for divorce settlements—by several million dollars.

Within moments of the verdict being read, the internal calculator in Hale's head began to whirr again. The numbers it spit out made him sick: he would owe Sheila $967.50 every day for the next 20 years.

"God, we heard about that at least a couple of times a week!" Ken Jones said.

In a loud voice, Hale would announce to everyone in the office upon his arrival: "Every morning when I get up, I know I have to make $967.50 to pay that (expletive.)"

The inevitable second-guessing about Ed Hale's decision to go to trial soon followed. Hale blamed himself for not being more forceful in detailing how Sheila had pleaded to be represented by Belsky, which he viewed as a key element in his downfall. ("She got amnesia," he'd say of Sheila in a withering tone.)

But to Shale Stiller and the rest of his legal team, there was no doubt the heretofore savvy businessman had been done in by his own impulsivity and a frantic attempt to save his wealth.

"This was one of the first colossal errors of judgment that Ed ever made," Stiller said. "And it cost him dearly.... If Ed hadn't given her this dumb (separation) agreement and they had the divorce action back in '84, she would have gotten half of $5 million. . .

"In other words, it's fair to say in the last legal action, she ended up getting more assets than Ed Hale had himself when the whole litigation began in 1984."

As part of the settlement, Hale was ordered to pay Stiller's fee of $275,000. Still steaming, he concocted another grand scheme: he would pay the fee in small coins. Just to torture his ex-wife's legal team one more time.

Lipsitz, the accountant, was called in to handle the logistics.

"I said: 'Ed, are you serious?'" he recalls. "He said: 'Absolutely.' But he didn't say it that nicely."

Lipsitz shakes his head and laughs at the memory.

"I actually had to call the Federal Reserve (and ask): 'How do you do this?' I said we need $275,000 in nickels, dimes and quarters. And the (answer) that came back was, it would take two armored cars to deliver it. And then it could potentially break the elevators.

". . . I think Sandler eventually said: 'Ed, it's not worth it. It's going to cost you $10,000 to do it.'"

Once Stiller got wind of the plot, he, too, called Hale and warned him not go through with it. Finally, the seething businessman calmed down enough to listen to the voices of reason.

Still, lashing out at Sheila's lawyers had been a typical Ed Hale reaction. Battered and bruised and rocked back on his heels, he was determined to throw one last defiant haymaker before going down for the count.

Fallout from the trial would continue for a long time, often with its own attendant drama.

For years after the trial, Jim Smith would hear about Ed Hale bad-mouthing him at dinner parties and in speeches to civic and business groups.

"He was making me the butt of his jokes," Smith says now with a chuckle. "He was making hay out of it. And knowing his personality, I think he was kind of proud that he had the biggest divorce settlement.... He likes being no. 1."

"No, I wasn't bragging about it," Hale says of those years. "Far from it. I just found the inequity of the settlement to be outrageous."

Years later, in 2002, when Smith was running for Baltimore County executive, a mutual friend persuaded him to meet with Ed Hale. Hale, after all, was a wealthy and influential Democrat with businesses in the county. And Smith, no matter his previous encounter with Hale, was a politician trolling for support and donor money.

The two sat down together in Hale's office. The conversation got off to an awkward start—at least for Smith. As the candidate listened impassively, Hale railed about how unfairly Smith had treated him during the divorce, and how the huge settlement awarded Sheila had nearly ruined him.

"Oh, I don't know, Ed," Smith replied, gazing around at the sleek furniture, plush carpeting and expensive paintings hanging from the walls. "It looks like you did pretty well for yourself.'"

That broke the ice. It was the perfect riposte to Hale's bluster, and it earned the businessman's respect. Eventually, Hale decided to back Smith in the race, and the two would go on to become good friends.

But perhaps the strangest repercussion from the divorce trial occurred years later when Hale sat down for lunch with Henry Rosenberg, the powerful, long-time head of Crown Central Petroleum Corp.

The meal had been arranged by Buzzy Krongard, the chairman and CEO of Alex. Brown & Sons. Krongard had heard that Rosenberg had been saying unflattering things about Hale around town, and he hoped the two captains of industry could hash things out.

The three men had hardly taken their seats in the Alex. Brown dining room when Krongard cleared his throat.

"I understand there's been some friction between you two," he began.

Hale sipped his iced tea, shrugged and said: "Nothing on my part."

But as the conversation continued, Hale realized the source of Rosenberg's irritation: the man was miffed that Hale's huge divorce settlement had eclipsed his own. (After splitting from his wife, Eleanor, in 1984, Rosenberg had been ordered to pay a settlement of $1.75 million, plus $275,000 in alimony per year.)

Hale was astounded. At first he thought Rosenberg was joking. *This is why you're ticked off?*

But when he saw Rosenberg was serious, Hale cracked: "Well, why don't you pay me the difference and I'll abdicate the throne?'"

Mercifully, the conversation quickly moved on to other topics.

But for Ed Hale, one thing was clear: his divorce—and the astronomical settlement it spawned—would continue to be an endless source of fascination in Baltimore for years to come.

# CHAPTER 9

## The Wizard of Oz Buys a Team

To watch Ed Hale at a Blast game is to watch a man emotionally whipsawed for the better part of two hours.

When the Blast scores, he throws a fist in the air and claps with delight. When the team surrenders a goal, he groans and covers his head with his hands. When a referee calls tripping on a Blast player, Hale's eyes become dark slits and he wails *"WHA-A-A-T?"* as if he's just witnessed the most bone-headed call in the history of organized sports.

For home games, he sits in section 110, some 15 rows up from the floor—there are no luxury suites in the boxy, charmless 52-year-old Baltimore Arena. The old NBA Baltimore Bullets played here shortly after it first opened as the Civic Center, and so did the Baltimore Clippers minor league hockey team. Over the years, so did the Beatles, Frank Sinatra, Bob Dylan, the Supremes, the Rolling Stones, the Grateful Dead, Led Zeppelin and Bruce Springsteen.

Pro wrestler Bruno Sammartino had folding chairs smashed over his head and Dr. Martin Luther King gave a fiery speech entitled "Race and the Church" here, and sometimes it feels as if the ghosts of 10,000 circuses, rodeos, concerts, tennis exhibitions, boxing matches, demolition derbies, lingerie football games and mixed martial arts bouts still haunt the drafty, cinderblock halls.

Hale is cordial when fans and friends stop by to say hi, but he's clearly focused on the game. This is no time for chit-chat. He wants to see his team win. And he wants to see his players hustle and scrap and give the fan's their money's worth, with the kind of relentless, blue-collar effort he's always demanded of his employees.

There's also this: Hale watches intently because he wants to *understand* the game, every facet of it, the nuances and strategy, what motivates the players, what doesn't --- just as he has with every other business he's ever owned.

But on this cold December night, in their 2013-2014 home opener, the defending Major Indoor Soccer League champions are on their way to absorbing a fierce 8-0 drubbing at the hands of the Milwaukee Wave.

Shutouts are rare in these frenetic, action-packed games, where scores of 27-13 and 25-9 are not uncommon. And right now Hale is mightily embarrassed.

His jaw seems to clench a little tighter and his frown deepens with each passing minute of futility for the home team. When the Blast pulls its goalkeeper for a sixth attacker with four minutes left, he mutters darkly: "We probably couldn't score with a *seventh* attacker."

When the game is over, he heads to the Blast locker room and listens in as head coach Danny Kelly delivers a blistering tongue-lashing to his players, who are slumped in their chairs and have the good sense to adopt the mournful countenance of 15 men that have just watched their homes burn to the ground.

"AN ABSOLUTE FUCKING DISGRACE!" is one of the kinder remarks Kelly will direct at his team.

Hale, leaning against the training table, looks on impassively as his coach's harangue approaches Earl Weaver-esque intensity in its volume, epic swearing and overall disgust for the pitiful effort just witnessed.

Then Hale heads quietly to the garage where his sleek black Jaguar is parked near the entrance, ready to whisk him to his Eastern Shore farm for the weekend. A loss used to eat at him for days, back when he was a new owner and wound much tighter. Now he bounces back in a few hours, having adopted a more philosophical attitude toward nights like this.

"It's not healthy to harbor crappy thoughts for too long," he says.

Hale first bought the Blast in 1989 for $850,000 from a group of Pikesville investors headed by Nathan Scherr. He hoped to establish himself as a bonafide sports team owner and therefore a potential buyer if an NFL expansion franchise became available to replace his beloved Baltimore Colts.

He had been a die-hard fan in the 50's, 60's and 70's, when the Colts ruled Baltimore and Memorial Stadium was known far and wide as the "World's Largest Outdoor Insane Asylum." And he'd never gotten over the pain that seared the city when owner Robert Irsay moved the team to Indianapolis—in the infamous Mayflower vans—on a snowy March night in 1984.

"What a coward, what a low-life Irsay was," Hale says, the words dripping with disgust. "There was nothing that galvanized the Baltimore community and Maryland like the Colts did. The farmers and aristocrats from the Eastern Shore, the Jewish community, the blue-collar folks from Dundalk and Edgemere, the wealthy people in the Greenspring Valley—everybody was crazy about the Baltimore Colts.

"When the season started, it was like Christmas every Sunday."

Hale didn't get an NFL franchise—the league snubbed Baltimore, with commissioner Paul Tagliabue famously suggesting the city should build a museum instead of obsessing about a football team. But Hale's purchase of the Blast staved off a possible franchise move to Cincinnati, making him a hero in the eyes of the city's leaders and indoor soccer aficionados.

It also changed his public profile dramatically.

"Even though I had all these monster businesses, no one knew who I was until I owned the Blast," he said. "I was like the Wizard of Oz, always in the background."

Being a recognizable figure in "Smalltimore" proved to be both good and bad for the ego, as he discovered almost immediately.

After an introductory press conference in '89 to announce the change in team ownership, Hale did an interview in front of his Clinton Street offices with long-time WBAL-TV sportscaster Vince Bagli .

"How's it feel to own the Baltimore Blast, Ed?" was Bagli's first question.

Hale, bursting with pride but nervous about his first live shot on television, was about to respond when a carload of longshoreman drove by. Hale's antipathy toward unions was well-known by then. Suddenly one of the longshoremen rolled down the window and yelled: "ED HALE BLOWS!"

Thankfully, that cheery welcome didn't make the 6 o'clock news.

But the fact was, Hale's ownership breathed new life into the Blast—and the league. Within a year, he was elected chairman of the MISL's Executive Committee and Marketing Committee, quickly becoming known as one of the most energetic and dedicated league executives.

"He was just a solid, no-nonsense guy—and he wanted to help," says Earl Foreman, the MISL commissioner at the time. "What distinguished Ed... as much as anything else: it was two for you and two for me. Ed had a cause and he would fight for it. But that cause would benefit everyone else as much as him."

(Years later, at a speech to the Advertising Club of Baltimore, Foreman called Hale the best owner he'd ever seen in any sport.)

Blast attendance held steady, with an average of 8,500 fans for home games. This was down from the 11,000 fans who packed the Arena in the heyday of indoor soccer in the early 80's, when the team was coached by the charismatic Brit, Kenny Cooper, and players such as Stan "The Magician" Stamenkovic and hard-nosed defender Mike Stankovic delighted the crowds.

But it was a respectable figure, given that the halcyon days of the sport were clearly over.

Still, Hale lost money, some $2 million in his first four years. And the Blast lost games, lots of them, making it a fairly miserable experience for a rookie owner.

Nevertheless, Hale fell in love with the sport.

He loved the fast-paced, substitutions-on-the-fly, end-to-end action that distinguished it from outdoor soccer, which he found boring. The blaring rock music, the goofy mascots, the non-stop promotions during games—he could live without all that. But he appreciated that the players were normal-sized athletes that the average fan could relate to, players from all over the globe who were educated, articulate and without the towering egos of NFL, NBA and MLB players.

These were players whom, he felt, fit in well with his long-standing "No Dickheads" rule. Loosely stated, the rule went like this: if you worked for Ed Hale and caused trouble by thinking you were bigger than the business or bigger than the team, you were gone—in a heartbeat.

The Blast found out all about this rule one day in the early 90's, when Cooper implored Hale to deliver a pep-talk to the team. The Blast was playing poorly, in danger of missing the playoffs. The players needed a kick in the butt. Cooper especially wanted Hale to light a fire under three Blast stalwarts he felt were under-producing: Dale Mitchell, Billy Ronson and Tim Wittman.

Hale was reluctant to single out players for criticism in a team meeting.

"If you have a problem with someone, you call him into your office and deliver the message privately," was how he operated. But Cooper was insistent.

All went well as Hale delivered his opening remarks and chided Mitchell and Ronson for their lethargic play. Then he started in on Wittman, the team's high-strung, fiercely-competitive defender. The Calvert Hall grad, leaning on crutches while nursing a bad knee, looked on sullenly.

"Timmy," Hale began, "you've had a lot of injuries, you're not practicing and people are taking exception to it . . ."

Which is when things started going... not so well.

"Fuck!" an enraged Wittman cried.

Then he began advancing on Hale and cursing him loudly before general manager John Borozzi eventually steered the volatile defender out of the room.

The sight of a badly-hobbled player trying to get at the owner was both surreal and comical. It brought to mind the hilarious scene in the old movie "Monty Python and the Holy Grail," where King Richard hacks off the arms and legs of the Dark Knight, who calls each severed limb a "flesh wound" and wants to continue their duel.

But no one was laughing now.

When Wittman was gone, Hale looked at the rest of the wide-eyed players and said: "Anybody have anything they want to add to that?"

The silence was deafening.

"Well," Hale continued, jerking his head in the direction of Wittman, "you just witnessed his last official act as a Baltimore Blast player."

Just like that, Wittman was a Dead Man Limping. And the "No Dickheads" rule had again been enforced with stunning swiftness.

By that afternoon, Tim Wittman was gone. He would soon sign with the San Diego Sockers as a free agent and help them win the championship the following season. (Ironically, 13 years later, Hale would let bygones be bygones and hire Wittman to be the new Blast coach.)

Even without players threatening to kick his ass, Hale discovered the life of a team owner was never dull.

When he traded David Byrne, a popular South African striker, Hale was hung in effigy by angry Blast fans. A middle-aged man who sat not far from Hale at home games even took to wearing a T-shirt that said: "Will Rogers Never Met Ed Hale."

"He would walk up and down the aisles and I would never look at him," recalled Carol Hale, a die-hard fan who still attends every home game. "'Cause I was afraid I would say something nasty. I didn't want to bring myself down to his level."

While the T-shirt drove his mom nuts, Hale found humor in the situation, going so far as to have his picture taken with the fan while flashing a goofy smile and giving the thumbs-up sign. And years later, when that same fan had a series of health setbacks and was confined to a wheelchair, Hale let him attend the games for free.

But by Hale's fourth year as the Blast's owner, the league—now called the Major Soccer League—was on life support.

Revenue was plummeting. Player salaries were out of control. Hale went to the players' union with an ultimatum from the owners: lower the salary cap or they would disband the league. When the union called their bluff, the owners voted with their pocketbooks and the league folded after the '91-'92 season.

But Hale wasn't out of indoor soccer for long. In the spring of 1998, he bought the Baltimore team known as the Spirit from businessman Bill Stealey for the fire-sale price of $100,000.

The Spirit was playing in the latest iteration of indoor soccer known as the National Professional Soccer League. Spirit games had been drawing 1500 fans to the Arena. But Hale restored the team's red and gold logo and brought back such theatrical touches as the giant soccer ball that descended from the ceiling for player introductions.

Season ticket sales increased by 50 per cent. The season opener drew 9,000 fans. This was a leaner and meaner operation than before: player salaries were a fraction of what they'd been in the glory days. Blast tickets sold for $7 to $15 and Hale figured he needed only 5,000-6,000 fans a game to break even.

Within a few years, the Blast became a league power, winning championships in 2003, 2004, 2006, 2008, 2009 and 2012. They were, for all intents and purposes, the New York Yankees of indoor soccer, although without the arrogance and Evil Empire overtones.

Indeed, Hale, with his deep pockets, willingness to share and determination to keep the oft-struggling league afloat, was no Darth Vader. As everyone in the league understood: what was good for the Blast was good for indoor soccer.

"For the last 20 years, he's kept indoor soccer alive in America," said Salvatore "Soccer Sam" Fantuzzo, majority owner of the MISL's Rochester Lancers.

"I believe if Ed had said at any point in time, that's it, I'm done, the league would have folded," said Blast general manager Kevin Healey. "But he was the driving influence."

In this second go-around as owner, Hale was a feisty and combative as ever, as a Blast player named Neil Gilbert learned first-hand in 2005.

Gilbert, 34, was a rugged defender from Argentina with a reputation as a loose cannon and cheap-shot artist. He was also a master at feigning injury with Oscar-worthy dives to the carpet in order to get a timeout and give his team a breather.

"He was known to be very skilled, but very crazy," Kelly said. "He's the type of guy, you love him when he's on your team, but you hate to play him when he's on the other team. Big, physical, strong, nasty, mean."

Gilbert was already on Hale's bad side for a number of perceived transgressions: showing up hung-over for practice, gambling heavily and living in a no-pets-allowed apartment with his German shepherd, with the landlord calling the Blast often to complain.

But things came to a head when Gilbert scored a meaningless goal late in a game when the Blast were getting their butts kicked. He then ran over to where Hale was sitting and launched into a bizarre—and obscene—celebration.

"He starts giving me the finger!" Hale recalled. "And he's mouthing 'Fuck you!' and making slicing motions across his throat."

Hale was still steaming at Gilbert's antics when the game ended. A couple of his friends invited him out for pizza, and he waved them off.

"No," he hissed, "I'm going to pick a fight with Neil Gilbert."

With that, he stomped to the Blast locker room and waited for the players to come off the field. Gilbert was the last one in. Hale ripped off his leather jacket and got in Gilbert's face.

"Ed said: 'You want a piece of me?'" recalled Kelly. "'Go ahead, take the first punch!' And they're like nose to nose. Gilbert kept saying: 'You're crazy! I'm not gonna hit you! You're crazy!'"

The two were quickly separated. A short while later, still furious, Hale was driving down Pratt Street when his cell phone rang. It was Wittman, now the Blast coach. Quickly, he explained that Gilbert hadn't directed his weird post-goal rant at Hale after all.

Instead, it had been meant for a couple of Brazilian fans sitting directly behind Hale, whom Gilbert accused of having thrown beer on him earlier.

Oh, Hale thought. Well, um, never mind with that "take the first punch" stuff.

At a practice a couple of days later, Hale sheepishly apologized to Gilbert. But Gilbert's actions had violated the "No Dickheads" rule too many times. He was soon let go, although the near-fight with

Hale had a galvanizing effect on the rest of the Blast.

"The reaction of the players," Kelly said, "was 'Holy shit! Our owner was willing to fight one of the toughest guys on the team!' That's the kind of owner you want to play for."

Still, since he first bought the team 25 years ago, Hale has prided himself on being a demanding—but not meddling—owner.

In fact, when Baltimore Evening Sun sports columnist Phil Jackman wrote in 1990 that the new Blast owner was a combination of George Steinbrenner, Donald Trump and Robert Irsay for threatening to rid the team of malcontents who didn't hustle, Hale was furious.

The comparison to the notoriously-boozy Irsay, who ran a beloved franchise into the ground and then packed it up like it was so much Tupperware and moved it to the city derided as "India-no-place," especially fried Hale.

After reading the column, he got Jackman on the phone and reamed him out a profanity-riddled screed.

"I shouldn't have put Irsay in there," Jackman says now. "That really boiled his ass. If I'd known he was going to take it so seriously... I (would) have left that out. It took me about 15 minutes to (realize): 'Geez, he's really pissed off here.'

"So I apologized," Jackman continued. "And I said: 'Why are you taking it (so hard?) Everyone knows Irsay's a drunken asshole."

Meaning: you're not anything like him, so no one's going to take the comparison seriously. But Hale was not appeased.

"Oh, you don't know Baltimore people," he told Jackman, who grew up in Massachusetts, but had lived in Baltimore for decades. "They read something in the Sun, (they think) 90 per cent of the time it's true."

These days, with the Blast receiving precious little media coverage and Hale's place as the indoor game's impresario secure—Fantuzzo calls him "the Godfather of Indoor Soccer"—Hale is no longer drawn into nasty spats with media types over how he runs his team.

But he seems every bit as interested in staying connected to the Blast as he was when he first bought the team.

After a win, Hale will invariably call Kelly to talk about the game and to give his impressions of which players played well and what the team did right, often prefacing his remarks with: "Look, you're the coach, but here's the way I saw it . . ."

"Sometimes I agree with him," Kelly says, "sometimes I don't."

After a loss, Hale tends to be more—how to put this?—inquisitive.

Then, according to Kelly, a typical conversation goes like this:

Hale: "What happened?"

Kelly: "Ed, we just didn't play well."

Hale: "Why not?"

Kelly: "We just... our fundamentals were off. Our passing was off."

Hale: "What do you mean? How is that possible?"

Kelly: "Some guys had a bad game, Ed."

Hale: "Who had a bad game?"

And on and on it goes. None of which seems to bother the Blast coach in the least.

"It's his team," Kelly says. "I appreciate the fact that he's hands-on in terms of wants to know. He doesn't tell me what to do. But he really wants to be part of the team, in terms of it's his company, 'How can I make this more successful, what can I do?' But he's never meddlesome or anything like that."

Nevertheless, no one in the organization doubts Ed Hale's competitive nature, or the value he places on winning—in every walk of life.

It's not by accident that a painting of a lion and gazelle is perched for all to see atop a file cabinet in the main hallway of the Blast offices in Rosedale.

Entitled "The Essence of Survival," the inscription reads:

"Every morning in Africa, a gazelle wakes up. It knows it must run faster than the fastest lion or it will be killed... Every morning a lion wakes up. It knows it must outrun the slowest gazelle or it will starve to death.

"It doesn't matter whether you are a lion or a gazelle... When the sun comes up, you'd better be running."

The Blast did just that throughout the entire 2013-1014 season. They hustled and scrapped so well, in fact, that they found themselves in the championship game against the Missouri Comets on March 16.

Win or lose, this was the last day they would ever play in the MISL. Hale had decided he Blast needed to get more "relevant." Therefore, he was already heading the effort to merge the Blast with teams from the Professional Arena Soccer League (PASL) to form a new, expanded league with a national scope.

The Blast players were pumped for the Comets. Having lost the first game of the championship series in Kansas City, they needed to win this game at the Arena and force a 15-minute mini-game to win the title.

In the pre-game locker room, Danny Kelly scrawled a cryptic note on the whiteboard: "Son, either with this or on this." It was what Spartan mothers used to tell their sons before they went off to war. Meaning the warrior should either come back victorious ("with this shield") or dead ("on this shield.")

Hale had something to say, too. He rarely addresses the team, but this was a special occasion. What he said was not quite as dramatic as the Spartan mothers' speech, but it was typical Ed Hale: brief, blunt and from the heart.

"This is the last MISL game ever," he began. "I want to win the championship one more time—the last time. I want to make sure all of you understand that. No fucking hugging these guys anymore please. It makes me want to puke when I see you doing that.

". . .Give it everything you got," he concluded. "I want to win this. I want to win it for Baltimore. This is the last MISL game. I expect you to go out and do it and I know you can do it. So stand tall and win these fucking games!"

Seconds later, the fiery Al Pacino pre-game speech from the movie "Any Given Sunday" blared over the sound system. The emotional trifecta had the desired effect: the Blast players looked as if they'd run through a cement wall to get at the Comets.

Baltimore forced the mini-game with a convincing 19-4 win before 6,447 frenzied fans.. But the Comets had heart, too. They scratched and clawed for an exciting 6-4 mini-game win that gave them the championship and ended the Blast's season on a shocking note.

Hale, Kelly and the glum-looking Baltimore players were classy in defeat, shaking hands and hugging the Comets and applauding during the trophy presentation. But by 9 the next morning, Hale was back at his desk in his Rosedale office, cranked up for another challenge. He spent the morning officially withdrawing from the MISL, overseeing the details of the proposed new league and surveying his roster as to who might return.

What followed in the next few weeks was a whirlwind of activity that had the Blast owner jumping on airplanes and meeting with MISL and PASL owners from all over the country, twisting arms to make deals, hammering out details of a merger and deciding on who the major shareholders will be.

It all culminated on an unseasonably cool May morning with a news conference at the Dockside Restaurant in Canton to announce the formation of a new 24-team league to be called the Major Arena Soccer League, or MASL.

As the TV cameras rolled and team owners, Blast officials, sponsors and media members feasted on fresh garden salad, pasta and chicken parmesan, Hale, the new chairman of the MASL, stood in front of a huge white map indicating that the new league would have teams in cities from Syracuse, N.Y., to Tacoma, Washington; from Turlock, Calif., to Brownsville, Texas, including three cities in Mexico (Tijuana, Saltillo and Monterey.)

The excitement in the room was palpable. There was even talk of national television contracts and sponsorship deals. What came through, too, was an almost missionary-like zeal on the part of the indoor soccer veterans to spread the game to new markets from coast to coast.

When the news conference was over, Soccer Sam Fantuzzo seemed almost giddy with the possibilities.

"This is a huge announcement for soccer in general in America," he said. "I mean, we had the '94 World Cup, then we had the announcement of the (formation) of MLS (Major Soccer League). And this is the next biggest thing.

"There's never been 24 teams organized in this country, playing (at a professional level)—it's never happened in soccer."

Behind him, Hale finished wrapping up the last of the one-on-one media interviews he'd do for the day. Fantuzzo watched him for a moment and smiled.

"In my opinion, Ed Hale is like the Lamar Hunt of indoor soccer," Fantuzzo said quietly, referring to the impresario and principal founder of the old American Football League and two outdoor soccer leagues. "Mr. Hale made all this happen. He pulled all the right strings. It's fantastic what he did for our sport."

What Hale had done for his hometown was not too shabby, either.

Now, for at least 10 nights and probably more each winter, the ancient mausoleum that is the Baltimore Arena would come to life with cheering soccer fans.

Jobs had been saved. Revenue would continue to flow into the city coffers. And yet another professional franchise would not skip town, headed for greener pastures.

All these years later, the Blast was still alive. Their new season would start in October.

And like the lion and the gazelle, Danny Kelly said, they definitely planned to be running.

The owner, Kelly knew, would have it no other way.

# CHAPTER 10

## "Mom, I Have All These New Friends"

Dennis Rasmussen seemed nervous—as nervous as Ed Hale had ever seen him.

It was March of 1991 and the handsome politician had recently lost his bid for a second term as Baltimore County Executive to Roger Hayden, a Republican. Now Rasmussen had shown up in Hale's office on South Clinton Street and was pacing back and forth, threatening to wear a path in the carpet.

"What are you doing here?" Hale asked finally. "And what does it have to do with me?"

The two were old friends, having gone to Essex Community College together in the late 60's.

Finally, Rasmussen looked up and blurted: "How would you like to become the chairman of the Bank of Baltimore?"

Hale wondered if his buddy had lost his mind.

"That's like asking: 'How would you like to become a space shuttle astronaut?'" Hale says now.

He was a trucker and a shipper and the owner of a pro soccer team, three businesses he ran with confidence and extensive knowledge of their inner workings.

But a *banker?*

All Ed Hale knew about banks is that he couldn't stand most of the stiff-looking "suits" who ran them, especially when they looked down on him and rejected him for loans.

Rasmussen explained that many shareholders were furious at the Bank of Baltimore—a bank with which Hale did business—for turning down an offer from First Maryland Bancorp to buy the bank for $17 a share.

The rejection had caused the stock price to plummet initially from $12 a share to less than $4. Ticking off investors further was that Baltimore Bancorp officials, specifically chairman and CEO Harry L. Robinson, had refused to even meet with First Maryland.

"My bank," Robinson had famously declared at the time, "is not for sale."

*My bank.*

The haughty words would haunt the otherwise genial banker for months.

To disgruntled shareholders, all of it signaled an astounding level of arrogance and incompetence. In their eyes, the bank had become this cold, imperious entity, no longer responsive to the needs and wants of its customers.

Now a group of dissident shareholders was looking for someone with the balls and deep pockets to take on the bank. They wanted someone not beholden to the financial establishment. Someone who didn't move in the social circles of bankers, who wasn't a member of their country clubs, who didn't sit on their boards and do business with them. Someone who, therefore, wouldn't worry about being scorned and ostracized.

Ed Hale fit the bill perfectly. Dennis Rasmussen recognized it right away.

"He's a good business guy, he's a straight shooter and he hates banks," Rasmussen had told the dissident investors. It was true: Hale had been outraged for years over all the red tape customers like him had to cut through in order to borrow money.

"The only time banks will give you a loan," Ken Jones recalled Hale saying for years, "is when you don't need one."

After listening to Rasmussen, the dissidents were sold on Hale. They asked Rasmussen to approach him about leading a take-over.

Now, staring at Rasmussen in his office, Hale asked: "What would I have to do in this take-over?"

"You'd have to win a proxy fight," the former politician told him.

"What's a proxy fight?" Hale replied.

Hale received a quick tutorial: the dissident group would attempt to convince shareholders of the 173-year-old bank to vote their shares in favor of their candidates for the board of directors. If those candidates received enough votes, they'd gain control of the bank.

Hale was immediately intrigued—for a number of reasons.

First, he owned roughly 10,000 shares of Baltimore Bancorp and was as miffed as anyone that his investment had lost money when the First Maryland bid was rejected. Now there was a chance to make even more money if the takeover was successful and he became the new chairman and CEO.

Secondly, Ed Hale viewed this as another challenge, another chance for the scrappy guy from Sparrow's Point to prove he was as smart and competent as anyone in the blue-blood banking establishment—the same establishment that had always turned its nose up at self-professed "red-neck truckers" like him.

Finally, there was this: Hale had tried to move all of Port East's and Hale Container's banking business—every account, including ship mortgages, land mortgages, truck and trailer equipment loans and credit lines, a total of some $26 million—from Maryland National to Baltimore Bancorp four years earlier.

After initially being assured by Harry Robinson that the board of directors would "rubber-stamp" the deal, it had instead been quashed. And Robinson had never returned Hale's phone calls or given him an explanation as to why he'd been rejected.

"I found out later on that some people in the bank thought I was in this grimy business," Hale said, referring to trucking. "My pedigree was not up to speed with them. 'Cause of where I'm from."

Being asked to take over a bank now, Hale thought, "was pretty heady stuff. And always in the back of my mind—*always*—was: 'I can take my revenge on these assholes for doing what they did to me for no good reason."

A Washington attorney named Dennis Gingold was brought in to school Hale on the mechanics of a hostile take-over. Hale put together a management team headed led by Charles H. "Buck" Whittum Jr., a former executive with Signet Bank. They filed to attack the bank on April 1.

But this was no April Fool's joke.

The bitter proxy fight would last six months. Hale spent $1.4 million of his own cash trying to drum up votes for himself and his new slate of trustees. No bank in the country had ever been taken over in a proxy fight, and he found himself in an uphill battle all the way.

The big New York investment houses sneered at the upstart trucker when he asked for their support. Hale remembered one hot-shot advisor to big pension funds, a man named Burt Denton, listening impassively from behind a bank of computers as Hale presented his credentials, then sniffing: "I ate popcorn at that movie. Get out."

At shareholder meetings, Hale was routinely vilified by audiences skeptical of his motives and put off by his background.

A stockholder from Connecticut set the tone at one particularly contentious meeting by pointing a bony finger at him and shouting: "What makes you think you can be the chairman of the board of this bank? You're not even *educated!* Who do you think you are!"

In the meantime, the bank took out full-page ads in the *Sun, New York Times* and *Wall Street Journal,* attacking Hale.

"We are dismayed that a group with little banking experience, led by Mr. Edwin Hale, has announced his intentions to gain control of your bank," read a letter to the shareholders in the May 9th *Sun.* "We believe the result would be disastrous for Baltimore Bancorps shareholders and depositors alike."

Even Hale's admirers were stunned at the audacity of his latest venture. More than a few of his friends wondered if he had finally bitten off more than he could chew.

"He was a trucker!" said Barry Bondroff, a CPA who had worked for Hale and was tapped for the new slate of trustees. "What did he know about banks! The only thing he knew about banks was that he had a bank account! That was it! He didn't know *anything* about it!"

Yet Hale, now 44, seemed to grow even more emboldened as bank officials took shots at him and nay-sayers waited for him to flop. The proxy battle, he recalled, "became a religious experience. I was on a mission."

The Hale group's strategy was to attempt to expand the board of directors by six members, and to run candidates for those six positions.

At first Hale appealed for support mostly to institutional investors—companies such as T. Rowe Price, First National Bank of Maryland and Legg Mason Inc., who were some of the banks biggest shareholders. These so-called "pocketbook investors" seemed most likely to seek a change in bank management after years of desultory earnings.

Indeed, a sit-down with the top corporate executives of First National proved to be a defining moment in the proxy fight.

Hale had gone to the meeting with little hope of getting the silk-stocking bank's support, fearing its top brass would look down on his pedigree. Nevertheless, he launched into a detailed description of what he planned to do once he took over the Bank of Baltimore, which included a legal and financial audit, as well as instituting a new culture of transparency from top to bottom.

"We're going to open the windows and let a breeze blow through there and let everyone know what's going on," he concluded.

The 15-minute spiel was met with a deafening silence. The executives stared stone-faced at the young businessman.

Finally, a distinguished-looking man named Jeremiah P. Casey cleared his throat. Casey was the chairman of Allied Irish Banks of Dublin, which had bought First National some years earlier. In a clipped brogue, Casey said: "Mr. Hale, would you mind stepping into my office for a moment?"

When the two men sat down, Casey fixed Hale with a shrewd gaze.

"Do you mind telling me why you're *really* doing this?" he asked.

Instantly, Hale could tell that the veteran banker had already surmised part of the reason.

"Well, I'll tell you, Mr. Casey," Hale replied. "I hate their guts at the Bank of Baltimore. What they did to me—when they turned down my loan and didn't have the courtesy to even call me back—I thought that was just patently wrong. And this is strictly revenge. But I can't say that in public."

Casey nodded.

In the next breath, he said: "Well, tomorrow, Mr. Hale, at 12 o'clock sharp, my CFO is going to call you at your office and tell you that we're giving you our proxy for our 400,000 shares."

Hale was flabbergasted. But he was also honored that a giant of the industry would have such faith in him and his cause.

"That was like five per cent of the total shares outstanding," he recalled years later. "After that, T. Rowe Price voted with me, and Legg Mason. And if they hadn't voted with me, I wouldn't have won."

In time, Hale expanded his lobbying efforts to include individual investors, too.

"I had a list of every mom and pop who had $10 all the way to the T. Rowe Prices," he would say later.

"What was unique about the Bank of Baltimore," Rasmussen recalled, "was that 48 per cent of the stock was owned locally. Or controlled locally, which is very unusual. Essentially we knew where 48 per cent of the stock was."

Predictably, Baltimore Bancorp soon brought in the big guns for the fight. In addition to the local law firm of Piper & Marbury, it hired the prestigious New York firm of Sullivan & Cromwell and its King Kong of mergers and acquisitions, H. Rodgin Cohen, the dean of Wall Street lawyers. It also hired a local PR firm to paint Hale as a cretin and detectives to dig up any dirt they could find on him.

"None of it," Hale recalled of the ensuing battle, "was for the faint of heart."

All of this elbowing and positioning by both sides was leading to what the *Sun* called "the biggest, nastiest corporate showdown of 1991" in Baltimore.

At the annual shareholders election in May, the atmosphere was tense and volatile. Concerned that things could get out of hand, the bank passed out a paper containing 11 "Rules of Conduct" in an attempt to maintain propriety.

Rule no. 9, for example, stated: "Derogatory references to personalities or comments that are otherwise inappropriate will not be permitted." One shareholder deftly maneuvered around this by telling Harry Robinson: "I'm going to be careful here and not call you arrogant, because that might get me kicked out of here."

Hale's message of change and openness resonated in the raucous setting of the Sheraton Inner Harbor Hotel ballroom. His group received enough votes to place six of its members on the board, although there were plenty of ballots on which were scrawled such niceties as "Hale, I'm voting against you, you're an asshole" and

"Who do you think you are? You're just an uneducated fool."

But a court ordered a new election, ruling that there were still questions about a number of uncounted votes.

So the battle for the bank dragged on.

As it did, Hale began to feel alone and isolated. Gingold was advising him on legal procedures and Whittum was his shadow CEO, but it was Hale doing the heavy lifting in the courting of shareholders. He was working 18-hour days, traveling constantly, often collapsing with exhaustion at night and sleeping on his plane.

And each time he appeared before the stockholders or bank directors, it had the feel of an axe fight.

Weeks after the May shareholders meeting, Hale appeared before the board. The meeting took place in the Bank of Baltimore's plush conference room, dominated by a polished table the size of an aircraft carrier deck and gilded portraits of somber-faced bank executives lining the walls.

Before Harry Robinson could convene the meeting, one of the board members, Richard Manekin, rose and stared at Hale.

Hale says he's never forgotten what came next.

"He said: 'Before we go on, I just want to say that your appearance here, Mr. Hale, and what you're doing to this institution, is beyond the pale. This offends the institution, but you personally offend me.'"

After Manekin sat down, an uncomfortable silence descended on the room.

Hale stood and asked: "Does anybody else have anything to say?"

When there was no answer, he continued:

"This is the United States of America. There are rules and guidelines that we use. And I'm abiding by those rules. I have every right to do what I'm doing. And I fully intend to win. I'm not doing this just for the pleasure of sitting here with all of you. I fully intend to win. And when I do"—here he gazed pointedly at Manekin—you're going to be the first one I fire."

Throughout the summer, Hale stepped up his "road shows" to big shareholders, getting more and more press coverage and putting more and more pressure on bank management.

In June, the beleaguered Robinson was ousted by the board of directors, receiving a $1.8 million golden parachute. Robert F. Comstock was named the new chairman and CEO.

Hale's group, meanwhile, received the support of T. Rowe Price and First National Bank, to the tune of some two million shares. Soon other big companies were pledging allegiance to Hale, too. He approached the August shareholders elections with growing confidence.

The Bank of Baltimore executives, on the other hand, sensed a disaster in the making. And their worst fears would come true.

As yet another contentious election got underway in the Sheraton's packed ballroom, Hale pulled off a masterful stroke of political theater.

A microphone had been set up in the center aisle for those who wished to speak. The microphone faced a stage, where Comstock, the board of directors, and the formidable H. Rodgin Cohen sat, looking out impassively.

When Hale took the mic, the crowd quieted down.

"Mr. Chairman," Hale said, "I'd like to speak to the audience. And I don't like having my back to everybody. Could I be permitted to go on the stage and speak to them face to face?"

The directors looked at one another uneasily. But what could they do? They couldn't say no to such a request without seeming dictatorial and petty.

"It was a great move," Rasmussen would say of Hale's tactic. ". . . He was talking to the shareholders, which was the whole reason everyone was there, because the board had ignored (them) for so long."

As was his wont, Hale kept his remarks short and sweet.

Glancing at the grim-looking men on stage—they were "ashen-faced," he recalled—Hale told the shareholders: "If you think by bringing in Mr. Comstock to replace Mr. Robinson that things are going to change, well, you're not that foolish."

Pointing dismissively at individual directors, he finished with a flourish: "If you believe *any* of these people... I'm going to bring in people to give this bank a fresh look with fresh ideas and transparency. I'm going to make this bank a much better bank than it is. I'd appreciate you voting for my slate."

On Sept. 9, Hale got the news he was hoping for. By 340,000 votes, he and his slate of directors had been voted in by the shareholders.

It was a singular measure of how far he had come. Ed Hale, the trucking and shipping magnate, was now the chairman of the board of the Bank of Baltimore.

He was both jubilant and relieved. The fight to take over the bank had been an exhausting, emotionally-taxing grind. And there were huge challenges ahead. First and foremost: the Hale team had been gathering intelligence for weeks indicating the bank was being crippled by bad real-estate loans.

But Hale was eager to get to work and begin tackling the problems. Still, it can safely be said that Hale's new career did not get off to the smoothest of starts.

When he phoned Whittum to say he was headed to the bank the next morning for his first visit as chairman, and wanted his new CEO to accompany him, Whittum told him that would be impossible, as he was headed off on a two-week sailing trip.

*Are you fucking kidding me?* Hale thought.

Things didn't get much better when he arrived at the bank. After shaking hands and accepting congratulations from downcast executives, Hale asked the president, Jack Haigh, to see the non-performing assets, or NPA's.

Haigh reached into a credenza and pulled out a stack of papers two feet thick.

Hale was shocked. "It was a who's who of big names in Baltimore," he would remember, the NPA's totaling some $238 million.

(One, ironically, belonged to Bernard Manekin, a prominent local commercial real estate developer, who would soon meet with Hale to ask for forbearance on the loan—it was granted—before moving the loan to another bank. He would also apologize for his son Richard's stinging remarks months earlier.)

By the end of the day, the new chairman was starting to realize the enormity of the task before him. Soon the bank would be operating under orders from federal regulators to raise capital. Still, Hale had never been one to shirk from a challenge, and this would be no different. Never had he faced a problem that he couldn't out-work.

His spirits were already lifting the next morning as he gazed out the window of his new office on the 25th floor of the old building at Baltimore and Calvert streets.

It was a beautiful day, clear and bright. Off in the distance, he could see the smoke stacks of Beth Steel and the bustling streets of the Highlandtown neighborhood where he was born, as well as the shimmering blue waters of the Inner Harbor.

It put him in a reflective mood. *I'm the chairman of the Bank of Baltimore!* he thought with wonder.

He decided to call his mother. Carol Hale had just listened to the news, which was still trumpeting her oldest son's latest stunning accomplishment.

"Is it true, Eddie?" she asked. "Are you really the new chairman of the Bank of Baltimore?"

Hale assured her that he was.

"What's it like?" was her next question.

"Mom," he said, a smile creasing his ruddy face, "I have all these new friends."

# HALE THROUGH PHOTOS

Baltimore mayor Martin O'Malley and Blast owner Ed Hale share a laugh at the trophy presentation at Canton Crossing following the team's 2002-2003 Major Indoor Soccer League championship season.

The 1st Mariner Bank Tower rises majestically across the Canton harbor in 2006. Work had not yet been completed on the 17-story, 480,000 sq. foot building; a giant crane is still visible to one side.

Hale and his father, Edwin H. Hale, at a family cook-out at the younger Hale's
Cockeysville home in 1989. For many years, Hale had a strained relationship with
his father, who died in 2002.

Hale and his daughters Alexandra (left) and Ashley at a wedding reception in
Rehobeth Beach, Del., in 2012.

Aerial view of the Canton Harbor and industrial surroundings before the development of Canton Crossing. Girlie Hoffman's lone rowhouse can be seen in the left-middle of the photo.

Hale and Baltimore Ravens' quarterback Joe Flacco shooting a commercial for 1st Mariner Bank in 2009. Hale was the star of many commercials built around the theme "We Built This Bank For You."

Hale singing karaoke in Taipei, Taiwan in 1990 with (from left to right) Gov. William Donald Schaefer, Owen Cole, president of First National Bank and Dick Trainor, Maryland Secretary of Transportation.

Hale shows off a 4-foot northern pike he has just landed at Hatchet Lake in
northern Saskatchawan, Canada in 2013. At left is a Cree fishing guide. Hale
has made many trips to Hatchet Lake Lodge, which lies in the middle of the lake,
caters to well-heeled customers and is reachable only by aircraft.

Gov. Robert L. Ehrlich joins Hale, Dept. of Business & Economic Developmnt
Secretary Aris Melissaratos, Dept of Planning Secretary Audrey Scott at the
ceremonial ground-breaking for 1st Mariner Tower in 2004.

Hale addressing the crowd at the groundbreaking for Canton Crossing in 2002. At left is an artist's rendering of the proposed $1 billion complex, which originally included an office tower, condominiums, restaurants, retail stores, a hotel and a 244-slip marina.

The Orient Trader barge docked at the Dundalk Marine Terminal in 1994. The barge, which Hale had built in Pass Christian, Miss., was 250 feet long and could hold 42 containers.

Hale's damaged Cessna Caravan amphibious plane after it crashed in Hunting Creek, just yards from his Easton farm, in 2002. Hale was returning from Baltimore; both he and the pilot suffered minor cuts and bruises.

Hale's yacht, the Exuberance, docked in Canton in 1988. The former America's Cup Committee boat was 85-feet long and had a mahogany hull and a smokestack. Hale often used it to entertain area politicians and visiting dignitaries, as well as Carol Hale's friends, the "church ladies.

Ed Hale poses with Miss USA beauty pageant contestants at a kickoff event at his
Easton, Md., home in 2005. Hale agreed to chair the event, which was televised
by NBC and held in Baltimore in 2005 and 2006, believing it would showcase the
vitality and beauty of his hometown, especially the Inner Harbor.

## ACHIEVEMENT IN SUBJECT MATTER AREAS

### SECTION I

| (See Page 1 For Code) SUBJECTS | First Term | Second Term | Third Term | Fourth Term |
|---|---|---|---|---|
| **READING** | C | C | C | C |
| Comprehension | | | | |
| Oral | | | | |
| Word Mastery | N | N | | |
| Use of Reference Material | N | N | N | |
| Independent Reading | | N | | |
| **LANGUAGE** | C | C | C | B |
| Written Expression | N | | | |
| Oral Expression | | N | | |
| Listening Skills | | | | |
| **SPELLING** | A | A | A | A |
| Basic Word List | | | | |
| Written Work | | | | |
| **HANDWRITING** | B | B | B | B |
| Legibility | | | | |
| Neatness | | | | |
| **SOCIAL STUDIES (Hist., Geog., Sci., Health)** | B | B | B | B |
| Basic Knowledge Facts | | | | |
| Skill in Use of Reference Materials | N | N | N | N |
| Sound Attitudes and Appreciations | | | | |
| **ARITHMETIC** | C | C | C | C |
| Understanding of Number System | | | | |
| Basic Facts and Processes | | | | |
| Accurate Approach to Prob. Solv. | N | N | N | N |
| **ART** | C | C | C | C |
| Expresses Ideas Creatively | N | | | |
| Shows Interest in Art Experiences | | | | |
| **MUSIC** | C | C | C | C |
| Participates in Activities | | | | |
| Shows Interest in Music Experiences | N | | | |
| **PHYSICAL EDUCATION** | B | B | B | B |

### SECTION II   Your child's achievement in relation to the standards for this grade:

| A CHECK (✓) INDICATES CHILD'S ACHIEVEMENT IN RELATION TO GRADE STANDARDS. | First Term | | | Second Term | | | Third Term | | | Fourth Term | | |
|---|---|---|---|---|---|---|---|---|---|---|---|---|
| | RDG. | SP. | ARITH. | RDG. | SP. | ARITH. | RDG. | SP. | ARITH. | RDG. | SP. | ARITH. |
| Better than Average | | ✓ | | | ✓ | | | ✓ | | | ✓ | |
| Average | ✓ | | ✓ | ✓ | | ✓ | ✓ | | ✓ | ✓ | | ✓ |
| Below Average | | | | | | | | | | | | |

2

Eddie Hale's sixth grade report card from Edgemere Elementary for the 1957-1958 school year. The report card featured a mixed batch of grades and a note from his teacher, Joe Waurin, concerning Eddie's behavior in class and lack of attention in discussions.

## PERSONAL DEVELOPMENT AND ADJUSTMENT

SECTION III

CODE: √ - Superior          No Mark - Satisfactory          N - Improvement Needed

| | | TERM | | | |
|---|---|---|---|---|---|
| | | 1 | 2 | 3 | 4 |
| PHYSICAL | Practices good health habits | | | | |
| | Is free from evidence of over-fatigue | | | | |
| | Has good posture | | | | |
| | Shows good sportsmanship | | | | |
| | Practices good safety habits | | | | |
| WORK AND STUDY | Works well independently | | N | | |
| | Works well with a group | | N | | |
| | Follows directions | √ | | | |
| | Makes good use of time | N | N | N | N |
| SOCIAL | Respects the rights of others | | | | |
| | Shows respect for authority | √ | √ | √ | √ |
| | Carries out responsibilities | | | | √ |
| | Takes care of property | | | | |
| | Obeys rules | √ | | | |
| | Is courteous | | | | |
| | Enjoys friendly relationships with classmates | | | | |
| | Cooperates in making group decisions | | | | |

SECTION IV

MAKES GOOD USE OF ABILITY

| | | | | | |
|---|---|---|---|---|---|
| | Reading | | | | |
| | Language | N | N | | |
| | Spelling | | | | |
| | Handwriting | | | | |
| | Social Studies | | | | |
| | Arithmetic | N | | | |
| | Art | N | N | | |
| | Music | N | | | |
| | Physical Education | | | | |

SECTION V          ATTENDANCE RECORD

| | 1 | 2 | 3 | 4 |
|---|---|---|---|---|
| Times Tardy | | | | |
| Days Present | 56 | 86 | 32 | 56 |
| Days Absent | 3 | 4 | 2 | |

CONFERENCE REQUESTED
X—Mark if Desired

| | | | | |
|---|---|---|---|---|
| Conference Requested by Teacher | | | | |
| Conference Requested by Parent | | | | |

Grade Placement
September 19 5 8 .

PROMOTED TO GRADE ___7___
RETAINED IN GRADE _____
WILL WORK WITH _____

Parent's Signature:

Term 1 *Mrs. Edwin Hale*

Term 2 *Mrs. E. Hale*

Term 3 *Mrs. E. Hale*

3

COMMENTS
Teachers and Parents

I wish you would speak to
Edwin Concerning his behavior in class.
For the past few weeks it has been
very bad and his attention to discussions
have been bad also. J. Hamin

I am sure you will
see a change in Eddie.
Both his Father & I were
very reluctant to hear this.

6-58
I enjoyed having Eddie in my
class. I want to take this opportunity
to wish him the best of everything.
J. Hamin

Other shot of Ed's report card. See above description.

Sen. Barbara Mikulski, Baltimore mayor Martin O'Malley and Congressman C.A. Dutch Ruppersberger in the audience for the groundbreaking ceremony of 1st Mariner Bank Tower in 2004.

Aerial shot of developed Canton Crossing with tower in background.

# CHAPTER 11

## Fresh Air Comes With a Price

It didn't take long, however, for Hale to realize that for the bank to move forward, some of his new "friends" would have to go.

All but three of the bank's directors, including Richard Manekin, promptly resigned. But more blood-letting was to follow. Hale was becoming increasingly dissatisfied with Buck Whittum, whom he found to be haughty, non-communicative and a pain-in-the-ass colleague to be around.

In the beginning of October, fed up with his CEO, Hale rapped smartly on Whittum's office door.

"Yes, who is it?" Whittum boomed in his stentorian voice.

Hale ducked his head in and said: "I just want to tell you your replacement is outside the door. And I want you to help him get acclimated."

The replacement was a man named Alan Lebernight. Hearing this, Whittum sputtered with rage.

"You can't do that!" he cried.

"Not only can I do it, I'm doing it," Hale replied.

When Whittum protested and said he would check with the board to see if Hale was within his rights, Hale answered: "I already did. And they're 100 per cent behind me."

Whittum stayed on for another six months, and then he, too, was gone, another victim of regime change.

In late November, Hale was summoned to New York to meet with a group of investment bankers, rating agency big-wigs and hedge-fund operators. The ostensible purpose was for the new CEO to deliver a "State of the Bank of Baltimore" address that would either encourage potential investors to loosen their purse-strings or confirm to jittery skeptics that it was time to dump their stock.

"But it was also so they could get a look at me," Hale says, smiling faintly at the memory. "Because I'm a trucker and not a banker or a corporate guy, was I going to drool when I do a speech?"

Instead, the presentation before a packed auditorium in an office building on Wall Street proved to be a huge hit—and a significant step forward for the bank and its rookie CEO.

After telling the audience how he planned to raise capital, get rid of bad loans and bring a new mindset of openness and community involvement to the Bank of Baltimore, Hale fielded a question from Harry Keefe, the dean of investment bankers with the firm Keefe, Bruyette & Woods.

(Ten years later, the firm's headquarters in the World Trade Center would be destroyed in the Sept. 11, 2001 terrorist attacks. Sixty-seven employees would lose their lives, including five of nine board members, as well as the co-CEO and chairman.)

"Mr. Hale," Keefe said, "it's very apparent that you have angered the landed gentry in Baltimore and the state of Maryland. It's not likely they're going to do business with you. How are you expecting to put money on the top line?"

Hale steeled himself. Should he give a politically-correct answer, that he would reach out to all areas of the community—including the noblesse who had tried so hard to discredit him—and work tirelessly to put the bank on good footing, ensure future growth, ingratiate itself to the good citizens of the Free State and blah, blah, blah?

Or with dozens of faces turned expectantly toward him, should he give the direct, no-bullshit answer that was already forming on his lips, practically screaming to be let out?

"I had to make a decision right there," he recalled. "Like—BOOM!—what am I gonna say?"

"You're right," he told Keefe, "it's unlikely I'll have any success with the people I unseated, and their friends and neighbors. However, I am very well-known in the Jewish community. In fact, I live in the Jewish community.

"And they do more in business, arts, culture and charities than all the blue-bloods do in Baltimore. That's who I'm going to direct my attention to, in order to do loans with them. I have a great deal of respect for them."

After the meeting was over, he raced to get the 4 p.m. Metroliner back to Baltimore. As the train pulled from the station, he received a call from Drew Larkin, a Bank of Baltimore board member.

"What did you *say* up there?" Larkin asked. "What did you *do?*"

"What do you mean?" Hale replied.

Larkin informed him that the bank's stock had just shot up from $9 to $11 in a half-hour.

The next morning, when Hale got to his office, the bank's stock-ticker page was on his desk, along with a note from the executive vice-president in charge of marketing.

"That must have been some speech," the note read. "The stock went up $34 million. That was a $34-million speech!"

By December, though, there was another headache to deal with: Hale was getting word that his lawyer, Dennis Gingold, and four members of the board had been meeting secretly and looking for ways to oust him as chairman. Gingold, it was said, had designs on being the new CEO.

Hale was furious. Loyalty was a character trait he prized among all others, which meant all five of the conspirators were dead men walking.

Right before a January board meeting, Hale asked the four directors to step into his office. He asked his young corporate counsel, Jim Gast, to come in, too.

"Don't bother fucking sitting down," Hale told the directors as soon as the door was closed. "I know what you're plotting to do. You're all fired. Get out of the building now."

Standing in one corner, Gast was shocked at the suddenness of the dismissals.

"There was no script," he recalled. "You're used to, as a lawyer, working with a script for your client... Your job is to think about the liabilities. But with Ed, there was no script.... When he needed to get something off his chest, he did."

Shortly after the board meeting, Hale ran into Gingold and fired him, too.

Over time, there were other scores to settle, some of far less significance. But settling them was no less satisfying to the hard-nosed businessman who never forgot a slight and embraced the belief that "revenge is fun."

Months into his new reign, Hale called the Greater Baltimore Committee, the organization of business and civic leaders dedicated to improving the local business climate.

Back in 1988, the GBC had refused to sell season tickets for the Blast, even though it had sold tickets for the Orioles. Hale's trucking and barge businesses made him the biggest employer at the Port of Baltimore, but that didn't seem to matter to the business group.

When Hale had asked why the GBC wouldn't sell Blast tickets, the curt response had been: "We're not disposed to do that."

Now, talking to a GBC rep as the new chairman of the Bank of Baltimore, Hale pointedly informed him the bank was no longer "disposed" to paying the committee's annual dues of some $50,000.

(In the years since, though, Hale has reconciled with the committee.)

But if the new bank chairman were ever tempted to think he was becoming a big deal outside the insular world of business, one incident in particular quickly disabused him of that notion.

It occurred a few months after he won the proxy fight, when he and two other prominent area figures were invited to Mount St. Mary's College in Emmitsburg, Md., as part of a fund-raising effort. The three had dinner with the school president and trustees, then took in a men's basketball game.

The Mountaineers' gym was packed. During an early time-out, the PA announcer intoned:

"Ladies and gentlemen, tonight we're honored to have with us the president of the Baltimore Orioles, Mr. Larry Lucchino; the Maryland Secretary of Transportation, Mr. O. James Lighthizer; and the owner of the Baltimore Blast and chairman of the Bank of Baltimore, Mr. Edwin F. Hale. Let's give them a big round of applause!"

What followed was a smattering of tepid clapping at best. More than a few fans seemed to stifle yawns.

Then the PA announcer continued: "And don't forget at halftime, we'll have a special performance by Fluffy the Frisbee Dog!"

Now the fans were on their feet, and the cheers and applause were deafening.

Sitting in the stands, Hale looked at Lucchino and Lighthizer and the three burst out laughing.

*Shows you what big-shots we really are*, Hale thought. *They could give a rat's ass about us.*

Over the months, the trucker and shipper had to quickly get up to speed on how to run a bank. But he proved to be a good learner and surrounded himself with astute and dedicated pros who knew the ins and outs of the business. Working hard, Hale and his team slowly nursed the bank back to good health, until even the federal regulators were impressed.

Three years after its tumultuous take-over, the Bank of Baltimore was sold to First Fidelity Bancorp of Lawrenceville, N.J. for $346 million in cash. Hale himself took home $6 million from the deal.

Now he was free again to concentrate on his other businesses.

There was also something else demanding more and more of his attention. And it involved serving his country in a way he could never have imagined.

# CHAPTER 12
## The Agency Comes Calling

Not long after starting his new career as a banker in the fall of 1991, Hale received an unexpected visitor to his lavishly-appointed office: Buzzy Krongard.

Krongard was a top executive with Alex. Brown & Sons, the venerable investment banking firm with offices in the same building as the Bank of Baltimore. Hale was aware of Krongard's growing reputation as a brilliant financial mind and "man's man," a legendary lacrosse player, former Marine and accomplished martial artist with a passion for firearms and all things military.

Hale also secretly wondered if Krongard, a Jew in the ultra-WASPy world of blue-blood banking, sympathized with Hale's status as an "outsider." After all, more than a few people were wondering what this rough-edged trucker was doing attempting to run a bank.

"Let's go for a walk," Krongard suggested.

"Why?" Hale asked.

"Just trust me on this," was the answer.

"I've got people coming to see me," Hale protested. "I can't leave."

But Krongard was not to be put off. "This won't take long. Come with me."

It was an unseasonably warm spring day and the two men headed out into the bright sunshine coatless. As they walked south, they passed others headed for the Center Club, the private dining club on the 15th and 16th floors of 100 Light Street favored by the titans of Baltimore business.

Hale had eaten there many times. But recently he had developed a growing disdain for the place with its hushed, white table-cloth elegance and obsequious service, as well as the often faux- back-slapping bonhomie of its patrons.

"I couldn't stand it because it was so pretentious," he said. "I would rather eat a peanut butter and jelly sandwich alone at my desk than eat there."

But lunch wasn't on the agenda this day. Instead, the two men continued to the Legg Mason building at Pratt and Light. They took the elevator to one of the middle floors and Krongard led them to a nondescript office. Quickly, they were ushered into a dimly-lit conference room, where some 10 men in dark suits stood waiting for them.

"What's this all about?" Hale asked.

"We're going to tell you," one of the men said. "But you have to sign this document first."

A sheet of paper was passed across the table. Hale glanced at it.

"What am I signing?" he asked.

"It's a confidentiality agreement," the man said. "It says you promise not to talk about this meeting."

Hale signed it without even reading it. It was an uncharacteristic move, but his instincts told him he had nothing to fear.

"I'm with Buzzy, whom I completely trusted," he explained years later. "I didn't think he would do anything that would get me in trouble."

A genial-looking man with blond hair introduced himself as David Miller. We're with the CIA, he said. After a moment or two of small talk, Miller made his pitch.

Would Hale consent to allow Agency operatives to gather intelligence overseas under the guise of working for his various businesses?

You're in a perfect position to help us, Miller told Hale. Everyone knows cultural and military attaches overseas are, in fact, CIA operatives. But you have a trucking company and a barge and shipping company with international ties. And you're also a banker, a real estate developer and you own a soccer team. Our agents could blend in easily pretending to work for you.

The Agency, Miller said, would create a fictitious new consortium for Hale's business called Parex, Inc. It would also set up a company web site—no small feat in the formative years of the Internet—that listed offices in Canton and Gstaad, the glittering jet-set mecca in the Swiss Alps.

"It was exciting to me," Hale remembered thinking as the plan was explained. "It was like if somebody came to me and said, 'We'd like you to set up a new business.' It gets my juices flowing. I thought: yeah, I can do this. Plus I'd always considered myself to be a patriot.

"So I wanted to help out and learn something new. And I was flattered they'd asked me."

Later, Hale was also told his help was desperately needed because of problems the Agency was having deploying operatives due to the so-called "Torricelli Principle," named after New Jersey's controversial Democratic congressman, Robert "The Torch" Torricelli.

This was the rule implemented by the Clinton administration that barred the CIA from employing sources who might have done something illegal in their past. To critics of the rule, this was like telling the FBI to infiltrate the Mafia without talking to any wiseguys. It was widely derided as "politically-correct spying."

Effective spies, noted Sen. Bob Graham of Florida, the head of the Senate Intelligence Committee at the time, "are not found in monasteries." Hale shared a similar sense of outrage over the new constraints placed on the nation's intelligence-gatherers. It made him even more eager to help.

Not long after, he would also learn that the unremarkable office at the Legg Mason building was known as a SCIFF (pronounced "skiff,") an acronym for a sensitive compartmented information facility where classified information was handled.

Hale's head was still swimming when the meeting broke up an hour later.

On the walk back to his office, he and Krongard were mostly silent. "I was just trying to digest everything I could," Hale said. But within weeks, mission plans were being implemented by the CIA and Hale was setting up dummy bank accounts and fake credentials for the spies who would be sent out under the auspices of his various businesses.

It was also in 1992 that Hale first heard a name that would make headlines all over the world after Sept. 11, 2001 and the murder of nearly 3,000 people in the deadliest attacks ever on U.S. soil: Osama bin Laden.

Bin Laden, Hale was told, was an international terrorist from a wealthy Saudi Arabian family who was high on this country's watch list. The CIA was tracking him. The hope was that operatives posing as Hale employees might be able to chronicle bin Laden's whereabouts and gather information on the money-laundering schemes in which he was involved.

Hale was now part of the shadowy CIA substratum of agents given non-official cover—known as NOCS and pronounced "knocks"—who typically posed as business executives. For the next nine years, Agency operatives purportedly working for him were dispatched to Uzbekistan, Cypress, Egypt, Lebanon and Jordan, among other countries where terrorists were known to operate.

Hale would be told the names of the operatives he sent out and their destinations, but never specific details about their missions. This allowed both him and the Agency to maintain the "plausible deniability" so critical to intelligence operations.

"All I asked the Agency to do," he said, "was to let me know when the mission was successfully completed. And they did that."

At the same time, Hale himself was going on overseas trade missions with Gov. William Donald Schafer to countries such as Norway, Poland, Denmark and Belgium and unofficially briefing his CIA handlers on all that he'd seen.

Inevitably, he attracted the attention of foreign intelligence agencies over the years.

On a trip to Israel in the mid-90's in his role as chairman of Israel Bonds for Maryland, Hale delivered a speech at the posh King David Hotel in Jerusalem. Shortly after, he was questioned by three grim-faced agents of the Shin Bet, the nation's internal security service, who wanted to know what he was doing in Israel.

Hale explained that he was there solely to promote Israel bonds, but the agents peppered him with questions. What kind of work did he do in the U.S.? Where had he been in Israel and what cities and sites did he plan to visit next? Where would his travels take him after leaving their country?

Finally, after a 30-minute interrogation, he was allowed to go. Later, he was told the same three agents had also visited the Parex office in Gstaad. Ironically, Hale himself had never been there, although a photo of him hung on an office wall.

"It's hilarious," says Kevin O'Connor, the Baltimore County Firefighters head who accompanied Hale on the Israel trip. "Here he's over there ostensibly to work for Israel Bonds. And he's over there doing fucking spy work! He's over there playing James Bond!"

Not long after the trip to Israel, the CIA concocted a mission that called for Hale himself to personally oversee.

He would fly to Georgia, the country in the Caucuses region

that borders Europe and Asia, to buy aging merchant ships and military vessels from the fleet of the former Soviet Union.

The ships would then be retro-fitted for intelligence-gathering purposes and turned over to the Georgian military. After, they would be used to disrupt terrorist activities in what was a major trade route for Al-Qaeda, the militant Islamic organization.

But just before Hale was scheduled to leave for the port of Poti on the Black Sea, David Miller contacted him. The trip was off. There had been an assassination attempt on Georgian president Eduard Shevardnadze in the capital of Tbilisi. The president's motorcade had been attacked by rebels wielding anti-tank grenade launchers and machine guns.

Shevardnadze was unhurt, but three were dead, including one of his bodyguards. The Agency felt there was too much upheaval in the country for the mission to proceed. And it was never resurrected—at least not with Ed Hale playing any kind of role.

After the Sept. 11 terrorist attacks on New York City and the Pentagon, Hale's services as a de-facto employment agency for spies were no longer needed.

"The gloves were off then," he said. "The thinking (in the intelligence community) was: 'They killed over 2,000 of our people? We're going to get them. And we don't care what anybody thinks, whether it's Mr. Torricelli or whoever. We're going after them.' That was the end of my career there."

The Agency would call again a few years later, asking if Hale would return in a similar role. But he declined after talking with Maryland Sen. Barbara Mikulski, who advised him that the climate in the Agency had changed and that NOCS were no longer receiving the support they had in the past.

(Mikulski, the chairwoman of the Senate Appropriations Committee, is understandably circumspect in talking on the record of Hale's CIA work. "I know he was involved and I know (the

Agency) asked him to help," she said early in 2014. "But that's all I know.")

Still, Hale looked back proudly on his service when he left the Agency. Years later, Krongard would express surprise that Hale never billed the CIA for his expenses. But Ed Hale was never in it for the money.

"I never got a fucking thing for it," he said. "The only thing I got out of it was Dutch Ruppersberger thanking me and Barbara Mikulski thanking me for my service. I just thought it was my duty as a citizen. If I could help, I'd do it."

Mikulski, in fact, was so impressed with Hale's service that at lunch one afternoon at Kali's Court in Fells Point, she had looked at him and gushed: "You and Buzzy Krongard and (New York mayor) Michael Bloomburg have panache!"

Working for the Agency had also re-kindled Hale's intense feelings of patriotism. As a teenager in Sparrow's Point in the 1960's, unsure of his future and at risk of being drafted and sent to fight in the jungles of Southeast Asia, Hale had loathed the Vietnam War.

"I hated Richard Nixon," he said. "Voted for Humbert Humphrey in '68. I had two friends killed in Vietnam right out of high school. Boom. Dead in three months.

"I thought: 'This is wrong. The Domino Effect? Old dudes telling us this is the way it's gonna be?' I just didn't believe them."

But Hale loved his country. And he believed—strongly—in the U.S. efforts in the Gulf War and Iraq War, and in the need to contain terrorism in the Middle East.

"So when they asked me to serve (in the CIA)," he said, "I felt good about it."

During the nine years he worked for the Agency, Hale told no one of his activities. Even Cindy Smith, his long-time secretary who arranged all his travel and appointments, suspected nothing about a secret life.

But his mysterious comings and goings put a strain on his second marriage, to Eileen Mahoney, which ended in divorce in 1996. They also damaged his relationship with Jennifer Gilbert, the stunning FOX-45 news reporter and anchor he dated on and off for six years.

"Over the years, I'd have to go places," Hale said, "and I couldn't tell Jennifer where I was going. She'd say 'Why can't we go to the farm?' or 'Why can't we go to this place or that function?' She didn't know what was going on. She just wanted to go off like a Roman candle."

Even after his work for the Agency was over, Hale told few people about it. Two he did confide in were his long-time friend, Mel Kabik, and another old friend, William Donald Schaefer, by then the governor of Maryland. Hale trusted both men implicitly.

He also revealed his CIA past to Tony Tranchitella when his old benefactor visited Baltimore and Hale gave him a tour of his luxurious penthouse digs in the 1st Mariner Tower in 2006.

"The man flew on 66 bombing missions," Hale said. Meaning here was a guy who would definitely keep his mouth shut.

But even though he had put it off for years, there was another significant person in his life that Hale was anxious to tell about his Agency years: Carol Hale.

He finally decided to do this over lunch one day in 2009 at his mother's home in Edgemere. Carol Hale had prepared Ed's favorite meal: pork roast, sauerkraut, mashed potatoes and broccoli.

In typical Ed Hale fashion, he didn't beat around the bush. The meal had barely begun when he cleared his throat.

"You know," he began, "I've done something throughout my career that I'm very proud of. And that is, I worked for the CIA as an agent."

At first, Carol Hale looked at her son and said nothing.

Finally she said: "Could you pass the broccoli?"

Hale was stunned. And the conversation quickly moved on to another topic.

Years later, still incredulous at his mother's reaction that day, Hale asked her: "Weren't you at all interested when I told you I worked for the CIA?"

"Oh, Eddie," she replied, as only a mother could, "you've done so many amazing things."

Spy work, Carol Hale had decided, was just one more to add to the list.

In 2013, Hale decided to talk about his CIA work for a forthcoming book about his life. But first he wanted to gauge the Agency's reaction to the project.

On a cold November morning in 2013, accompanied by a former *Baltimore Sun* columnist now writing his biography, Hale boarded a train for Washington D.C. to meet with his old handler, David Miller.

The meeting took place in a conference room of Torch Hill Investment Partners, a private equity firm that invests in companies with roles in law enforcement, defense, intelligence and security-threat assessments.

The three men were joined by Stephen R. Kappes, the former Deputy Director of the CIA, now a partner and chief operating officer of Torch Hill. Steve Kappes had been a legendary—and controversial—figure in the Agency until his retirement in 2010.

A career clandestine officer, he had directed the CIA's extraordinary-renditions program from 2001-2004, in which suspected terrorists were kidnapped and whisked to secret locations for detention and interrogation, allegedly including torture.

Even at age 62, Kappes, a former U.S. Marine officer, looked extraordinarily fit. He had broad shoulders that tapered to a narrow waist and huge hands, and still looked capable of snuffing out a man's life with a soup spoon. He wore a close-cropped mustache and beard and fixed the others with a penetrating gaze as he spoke.

Both Miller and Kappes expressed misgivings about Hale's

Agency work being mentioned in any biography. And they warned him of possible repercussions. If he still did business in Europe and Asia, they said, those businesses could be harassed by government officials who might read the book and conclude he still worked for the CIA. And Hale himself could be detained and questioned—maybe even arrested—if he traveled overseas.

You definitely can't go to Moscow, he was told, as the possibility existed that he could be held in exchange for a Russian intelligence operative being held in the U.S.

Hale replied that he no longer did business in foreign countries. As for himself, he added, the only hotspot country he planned to visit again was Israel, this time possibly with his grandchildren.

Miller and Kappes were quickly learning what dozens of others had learned about Ed Hale over the years: once he'd made his mind up to do something, there was little use in trying to talk him out of it.

"I know you're going to do this," Kappes said toward the end of the meeting, referring to Hale mentioning his Agency service in the book.

Hale nodded. There was, he felt, no longer a need for secrecy about his activities. He would divulge no operational methods that would hurt the Agency or compromise the safety of any past or present agents.

Why, just a few weeks earlier, Hank Crumpton, the longtime CIA officer who had led the U.S. response to 9/11 in Afghanistan, had come out with a tell-all book, "The Art of Intelligence: Lessons for a Life in the CIA's Clandestine Service." And this was after Crumpton had appeared on CBS's "60 Minutes" a year earlier, revealing to correspondent Lara Logan how the CIA had toppled the Taliban and found bin Laden two years before the 9/11 attacks, only to see its plan to assassinate him shot down because of the waffling of the Clinton administration.

No, Hale concluded, there was no earthly reason to keep silent any longer about his own modest contributions to the war on terror.

Even as the meeting ended and everyone shook hands and he headed out to the bustling mid-afternoon traffic, you could read it on his face: Ed Hale was at peace with his decision.

# CHAPTER 13

## Back in the Game

In the winter of 1991, the organizers planning the annual charity auction for Big Brothers & Big Sisters of Maryland hit upon a brilliant idea: the grand prize would be an evening out with the handsome multi-millionaire chairman of the event, Ed Hale.

Included were a limousine ride to Hale's yacht, dinner and a cruise around the harbor, and a chance to take in a Blast game with the team's owner himself.

Now, sitting uncomfortably on a stage as the bidding started, Hale evinced all the joy of a man being led to the gallows.

*Why did I agree to this?* he kept asking himself. *I must be nuts.*

In true Hale fashion, however, he had prepared himself for any eventuality. Especially the Doomsday Scenario: a roomful of skeptical women, many buzzed on a few glasses of wine, shaking their heads and whispering to each other: "Are you kidding? I wouldn't bid two cents for this guy."

His contingency plan for avoiding humiliation was simple.

"I had a woman I knew in the back of the room," he recalled. "And we had hand signals arranged—you know, like a third base coach in baseball? If either no one was bidding and it was getting embarrassing, or some real dog was ahead in the bidding, I'd give her a signal and she'd start bidding like crazy."

But the bidding was enthusiastic and an attractive woman named Diane Allen eventually won with a bid of $1,350. On the appointed evening out, Hale and Allen had a perfectly nice time together as the Blast owner, now over the stress of being gawked at and sold off, turned on the charm.

"I found him very... distinguished," Allen later told the Baltimore *Sun*. "There's nothing snobbish about the man. I like a man who's sort of shy."

*Sort of shy?*

By this point in his life, Ed Hale was about as shy around women as that other renowned wallflower, Warren Beatty.

After his divorce from Sheila Thacker, Hale had sworn off marriage, telling everyone: "I'm just not good at it." Asked if he could be monogamous, he'd joke: "I can. But I'm not fanatical about it," a view he would eventually renounce as he saw more and more of his friends in loving long-term relationships.

Now he was back in the dating game after emerging from a stormy on-again, off-again relationship with Michele Gutierrez, the mother of his two daughters, a relationship that had left emotional scars on everyone involved.

In the few years they had lived together in the mid-80's, the bickering and fighting in the household had taken on epic proportions.

"The only true memory I have of growing up of my parents is my mom crying a lot," Hale's oldest daughter, Ashley Flamholz, would say of those years. "I remember her crying all the time and being unhappy all the time. I don't have memories of us going places together at all. It's almost as if I don't remember them being together."

Hale was working long hours, and the stress of juggling his trucking, shipping and banking responsibilities made him something less than a warm and fuzzy dad in the six years he and

Michele were together.

"We were terrified of pissing him off in any capacity," Ashley remembered. "The smallest of incidents—he would yell and do this grumble thing with his face, and it would scare the shit out of us. When we did something bad, we were called to the den. Leading up to that moment was *the* worst time *ever*. It made you feel this big."

"I was always daddy's little girl," says Alexandra Hale, Ed's youngest daughter. "I looked up to him... (But) I definitely resented him for always being so busy."

Yet even after his split with Michele, Hale had always been a strong presence in his daughters' lives, attending their sporting events in high school, buying them their first cars and paying for their college educations at Goucher in Baltimore County and Penn State.

"But he never, ever spoiled us," says Ashley, now 30 and married with an infant daughter, Avery. "My brother had a totally different upbringing. He had the house, the parties, the car. He was a total rich kid. My sister and I did not have any of that. He bought us Toyota Corollas. He didn't take us on shopping sprees. We were always getting made fun of for not having nice clothes."

(Hale takes issue with this, insisting he paid Michele $200 a week for each daughter's living expenses, and that their mother failed to give the money to the girls.)

"But he paid for Goucher at $46,000 a year," Ashley continues, "and I feel spoiled in (that) sense... I remember him being extremely encouraging and wanting to know when we were getting our grades ... Anytime we've ever done anything to accomplish something, he's always been extremely proud. And my father has exceeded my expectations as a grandfather. The way he lights up when he talks about Avery and when he's around her warms my heart."

One of his proudest moments came when Alex, now 27, received her graduate degree from Towson University—especially since she'd been taken aback after her undergraduate days when her father had informed her that he wouldn't be footing the bill for any further education.

"It was kind of a rude awakening," she says now. "I really, really resented that I had to pay for grad school. (But) I almost thank him for it now, because I learned a lot. I learned I had to work hard. I know he had to work really hard for everything he got."

In recent years, Ed Hale began opening up more and more to both daughters, sharing stories about his successes and disappointments in both business and life. It was clear, too, that he wanted to spend more time with both, and both women say their relationship with their father is healthy and fulfilling after years of tumult.

"I look at my dad now as a much more patient, calmer person, not as hot-tempered as I remember him growing up," Ashley says.

Ed Hale's relationship with his son, Eddie Jr., has also begun to heal after years in which the two didn't speak to each other. Most of the acrimony, says Ed Hale, centered around Eddie's first wife, a woman named Beth Petr whom both Ed and Sheila Thacker regarded as an unfit wife and mother for the couple's three sons.

"I am not a role model," Hale says now. "But this woman was the *worst*."

Eddie Jr. is now 47, a successful trucking executive in his own right in Baltimore, who has since remarried. But the elder Hale says his disapproval of his son's first wife was so deep that "I have it stated in my will that, until eternity or infinity or whichever is longer, Beth will never get one penny of my estate."

Despite his own rocky first marriage, Ed Hale took the plunge once again in 1993. This time he married Eileen Mahoney, a stunning brunette from Washington, D.C., who worked as a secretary for Port East and caught his roving eye.

Eileen was smart, funny, sophisticated—and, in keeping with a pattern, 14 years younger. Hale's friends thought he had finally found a soul-mate. So did Hale, who admitted to everyone that he was in love.

A die-hard Redskins fans, Eileen would go around the house muttering "God dammit!" whenever her team lost and the Ravens won and her husband was gloating insufferably. It was a private joke they both enjoyed. But the jokes stopped and the marriage ended in divorce a few years later after she went sky-diving against Ed's wishes and broke her foot.

"After that," Hale recalled, "it was like: what's next? *Enough already!*"

Soon, Hale was again seen squiring a bevy of young lookers around town. But that ended for a time in August of 1998, when he first laid eyes on Jennifer Gilbert, a beautiful and brainy reporter for WBFF-TV (FOX 45) in Baltimore.

This was at a fundraiser at a local banquet hall for William Donald Schaefer, who was now running for state comptroller. Hale was serving as Schaefer's finance chairman when he spotted Gilbert across a crowded ballroom, sunlight from an overhead window shimmering off her hair and her blue floral chiffon dress.

He was transfixed, struck by what the Sicilians call "The Thunderbolt."

"She was absolutely, breathtakingly gorgeous," Hale recalls. "You know that scene in 'The Godfather' where Michael sees Apollonia for the first time and is instantly smitten? That's how it was for me."

Gilbert was working the event for her station and the two made small talk about politics for a while. But when her photographer wrapped up and it was time to leave, Gilbert, a poised 29-year-old who had graduated from Northwestern's prestigious Medill School of Journalism, felt something, too.

"I remember walking away thinking: 'Did something just happen there?'" she recalled.

Apparently it had. She made sure to be covering Schaefer's

headquarters on Election Night in mid-September, where the two had another long conversation and Hale told her: "By the way, I'm a really fun guy if you just want to hang out."

"Shortly after that," Gilbert recalled with a laugh, "I don't know what possessed me to do this, but I went to a floral shop and I got a single yellow rose. I sent it to him with a card that said 'In friendship' and I signed my name.

"After that, we got together for dinner and drinks, and one thing led to the next and it was like wild horses couldn't have driven us apart."

A torrid romance followed. The two connected on many levels. Gilbert herself had come from a modest background. Her father had been a steelworker and her mother a hairdresser, and she had grown up as an only child on a farm in southern Pennsylvania where her grandfather was born.

When she was a sophomore in high school, the NBC news anchor Jessica Savage died when her car ran off the road and plunged into a canal in a rural part of Bucks County, Pa. Reading a magazine article about Savage's career shortly after the accident had helped convince Gilbert that journalism could help her escape the often-claustrophobic atmosphere of her own small town.

Now, the more she got to know Ed Hale, the more she found herself engrossed by the narrative arc of his life.

"He had shared with me a great deal about his childhood and upbringing and his roots," Gilbert remembered. "And to see that he had come from there and risen to there was really extraordinary. I was very fascinated and in awe of that and curious. I wanted to know how he did it every step of the way."

Soon the powerful business magnate and the glamorous television personality were a sought-after couple for civic and charitable events all over town. But juggling their demanding careers and endless social obligations was exhausting.

On the weekends, the couple would retreat to Hale's farm on the Eastern Shore to decompress. There, during hunting season, Gilbert discovered another intriguing side to her boyfriend.

"I'd get up on a Saturday morning at a reasonable, civilized hour, like 8:30 or 9," she recalled. "The kitchen table would be full of guys who had been up since, like, 4 and had already been out hunting and were coming in for breakfast.

"And sitting at that kitchen table could be anyone from a CEO of a major corporation to the guy who paves driveways down the street. And they were all sitting there with this common experience around Ed Hale's dining table. That was always amazing to me."

The relationship between Hale and Gilbert wasn't linear; it lurched in fits and starts for some five years. But Hale came to trust her and confide in her and enjoy her company—enough, even, to turn down a dinner date with one of the sexiest movie stars on the planet.

In 2002, Hale received a phone call from his friend, James D'Orta, who had served on the Medstar board with him. D'Orta was a prominent Georgetown doctor, social gadfly and the founder and CEO of a physicians consulting firm based in Washington, D.C.

He was also the nephew of Cubby Broccoli, the film producer best known for the James Bond movies.

Now D'Orta was calling with an unusual proposition—to say the least.

"How would you like to be Halle Berry's dinner date?" he asked.

"Count me in," blurted Hale.

D'Orta quickly explained that Berry had just wrapped up shooting "Die Another Day," the latest Bond flick, starring Pierce Brosnan.

(The movie would go on to be forever etched in the minds of male viewers for a scene of a sizzling Berry emerging from the surf in a skimpy orange bikini, an homage to a similar scene that starred

Ursula Andress in a dazzling white bikini in the very first Bond movie, "Dr. No.")

Now, D'Orta went on, he was having this big charity fundraiser at his swanky Georgetown mansion, the former home of W. Averill Harriman, the late New York governor, diplomat and Democratic leader, and Pamela Harriman, his socialite wife.

Supreme Court Justice Antonin Scalia was also on the guest list, D'Orta told Hale, along with a couple of U.S senators and a stray ambassador or two. But it was the gorgeous Halle Berry providing the real star power. And since she was in the process of divorcing her husband, D'Orta was trying to match her with an interesting companion for dinner.

And Ed Hale was *definitely* interesting.

*Oh,* Hale thought, *I guess I could help the poor dear out . . .*

When he hung up with D'Orta, Hale was not delusional. He realized this was simply going to be dinner with Berry—no big romance was about to blossom. Nevertheless, he was practically giddy at the thought of escorting a big Hollywood star and the wow factor that would have with his friends.

"I was going to have a press conference the next day and announce: ED HALE FROM EDGEMERE HAD A DATE WITH HALLE BERRY!" he would joke years later. "That's what I *wanted* to do. But I kept it quiet."

Well, sort of quiet, anyway.

But somehow Gilbert found out about the invitation and asked him not to attend the soiree with Berry, saying it would hurt her too much. And Hale had too much respect for her feelings to do that.

When he called D'Orta back to cancel, the physician was incredulous.

"Let me get this straight," he said. "You're turning down a date with Halle Berry? *What?* Eddie, can we start all over again? This is one of the most beautiful, dynamic women on the planet!'"

But Hale's mind was made up. And a chance to have one of the greatest conversational openers of the New Millennium ("Ever tell you 'bout the time I went out with Halle Berry?") was gone forever.

Within a year, though, Hale's relationship with Gilbert was also reaching a dead-end. She was looking for more of a commitment from him, and he wanted no part of that.

*Commitment?* The very word could make Hale's palms sweat and his eyes twitch.

Nevertheless, one fine spring morning, while the two were approaching the Chesapeake Bay Bridge on the drive back to Baltimore from the farm, Gilbert gently broached the subject of marriage. It was something she'd been thinking about for some time.

*Oh, God*, Hale thought. *Here we go.*

But he said nothing, letting Gilbert continue on the topic until they reached the very top of the bridge's west-bound span.

Then gazing around at the panoramic view, the white sailboats dotting the cerulean water and the tankers emerging from the mist in the distance, he exclaimed: "Jesus Christ! Look at all the ships out there!"

Gilbert, no dummy, did not bring up matrimony again. And within weeks, the two had agreed to go their separate ways.

"I wanted more," from the relationship, Gilbert would say later. "And he knew that. And to his credit, he never led me to believe there would be more. It was always very straightforward. It got to the point where he was going one way and I was going the other. So that was the end."

No, Ed Hale was done with marriage—seemingly for good.

"You have to know your limitations," he would tell friends. "I may be a good guy to hang out with. But getting married and all that... nah."

Still, he was hardly done with romance, pursuing it with a parade of comely young women to the great delight—and envy—of many of his male friends.

"It's the American Dream in my book!" says longtime Hale buddy, Marty Bass, the WJZ-TV weatherman. "Why not, if you're a good-looking, successful guy and you're a great conversationalist and someone's interested in you? Why *not?* You're free!"

Which didn't prevent other pals from teasing him unmercifully about the age differential in his choice of dating partners.

Some years ago, at a party at Hale's ritzy penthouse condo at Anchorage Tower in Canton, Edie Brown and a friend happened to pass his bedroom and noticed the bed was unmade.

Hale confessed to having had a girlfriend over the night before, and not having had time to tidy up after she left.

"Did you give her her Teddy bear and send her back to school?" Brown asked sweetly.

Family members were often far less sanguine about Hale's May-December dating habits, however.

"Can you imagine showing up with someone 25 years old?" Barry Hale said not long ago. "... It's an enigma. It's funny, but it's sad. That was him and he's made no bones about some of this stuff. And that confounds all of us."

Ed Hale has always found his brother to be "too judgmental" about both his social life. And after many years, Ashley Flamholz, 29, and Alex Hale, 27, say they've come to terms with their father's well-known predilection for courting younger women.

"I struggled with it until probably last year," Alex Hale said in 2014. "He's 67 and he acts like a 25-year-old guy I would see in a bar!"

"It doesn't bother me because it makes him happy," Ashley Flamholz says. But before she went off to college" It definitely bothered me. I was like: 'That's gross.' It was just weird, because of how old he was. (But) it's something I've learned to accept."

As it happened, Hale's interest in beautiful young women and his unabashed boosterism for his hometown all converged in 2004 when he fielded a call from then-Baltimore-mayor Martin O'Malley.

O'Malley was attempting to bring the Miss USA pageant to town after it had been rotating among various cities. This would be an economic boon to the city and a major television event on NBC that could help turbo-charge tourism. Sponsorships would be critical for the event's success, which meant O'Malley desperately needed the support of the local business community and high-powered executives like Ed Hale.

The mayor didn't need to do a lot of arm-twisting to get Hale signed on as chairman.

"I remember calling him up and saying: 'Ed, I have a big favor to ask,'" O'Malley said. "He said 'Sure, what is it?' And I said 'Miss USA.' He said: 'I'm in.' I said: 'Don't you want to know what I'm asking you to do?' He said: 'I'm *in*.'"

At a news conference at the Hippodrome Theater to announce that the pageant had landed in Charm City, Hale gushed about what a wonderful event this would be for Baltimore, how it would showcase its vitality and beauty, especially that of the world-renowned Inner Harbor.

"As for me," he added with perfect comedic timing, "I've been training my entire life for this job."

The line brought down the house. But the way he went about his duties as chairman, it almost seemed as if he *had* prepared for years.

Hale immersed himself in the logistics of putting on a first-class beauty pageant, consulting often with Miss USA's billionaire owner, Donald Trump, whom he grew to like. He also took it upon himself to arrange much of the entertainment for the contestants when they were in town.

A few days before the contest took place the following April, Hale held a reception for all the women at his sprawling farm in Talbot County. After a morning of shopping and sight-seeing in nearby St. Michael's, the contestants arrived by an old-fashioned paddleboat in the river behind his house, with NBC cameras rolling.

There, waving to them from his veranda, was their distinguished host, Ed Hale. Also on hand, enjoying beers and cocktails, were some 200 of his male friends and business associates, Hale having eagerly spread the word that 51 of the most ravishing women on the planet would de-camp at his place that afternoon.

As the boat prepared to dock, Hale stood, looked at his friends, and said: "OK, let's go down and greet them."

"He starts to walk and he goes about 10 steps and turns around—and nobody's walking with him!" Bass recalled. "So he says: 'What is it about this that you guys don't get? Let's *go!*' It was like: 'The best-looking women in America are getting off that boat! And you're *standing* here?'"

In short order, the men dutifully assembled on the riverbank, flashing big goober grins and waving awkwardly, their eyes popping out of their heads as they beheld the dazzling beauties before them.

Watching his spellbound friends, Hale could only shake his head.

"The boat is about 50 feet away," Bass recalled. "The NBC cameras are shooting all this. And Ed looks around at us and says: 'I want to tell you guys something. If assholes could fly, this would be an airport.'"

The reception was a resounding success and the network got all the background footage it needed of the nubile contestants frolicking everywhere on Hale's property.

Just before the women were scheduled to board busses to return to Baltimore that evening, one of their chaperones came to Hale with a request.

Many of the contestants, the chaperone explained, had recently taped an appearance on the NBC game show "Deal or No Deal," hosted by Howie Mandel. Now the live version of the show would be on soon.

Would Hale mind if they all stayed to watch it?

"Let me get this straight," he replied, deadpan. "You want to know if 51 of the most beautiful women in the universe can hang out and watch TV?"

Soon, Hale was basking in the other-worldly sight of dozens of gorgeous women clustered around television sets all over his house, including the master bedroom.

A few minutes after the show started, Hale received a phone call. It was from his son, Eddie Jr., who was on a business trip to Florida.

"Dad," Eddie said excitedly, "turn on the TV! The Miss USA girls are on!"

Hale stifled a laugh and quickly put the call on speaker-phone.

"Girls," he boomed, "say hello to my son, Eddie."

"*HI-I-I-I, EDDIE!*" responded a sultry chorus of voices.

As he had so many other times in his life, Hale could only shake his head at the surreal circumstances he found himself in and think: you can't make this stuff up.

# CHAPTER 14

## "We Built This Bank For You."

After selling the Bank of Baltimore, Ed Hale, ever restless, was looking for a new challenge.

He had enjoyed his time as a banker and learned much about the industry and corporate governance in his three years as chairman. In May of 1995, he made another career-defining move: he bought four branches of MarylandsBank, a humble thrift with $25 million in assets, and started 1st Mariner Bank.

"We're doing something today that I've been wanting to do since the Bank of Baltimore was sold," the new chairman and CEO announced at an introductory news conference. "And that is, form a locally-owned bank here in Baltimore that has roots in the community."

As a trucker, Hale had had such bad experiences with banks, including the Bank of Baltimore, that the memories of how he'd been treated still galled him.

He was convinced that, for the most part, the big, soul-less, out-of-town commercial banks treated their customers—especially working-class folks—with contempt.

Often, he recalled, when he dealt with banks for his trucking business, "you couldn't even get to a person who could give you a discernible answer—and I was a big borrower—on whether or not they could loan you money."

The humiliation of groveling for a loan would fill him with dread in the weeks before he officially applied for one.

"I'm getting my knee-pads on and going down to the bank," he'd say bitterly on those occasions.

But 1st Mariner, Hale vowed, would be different.

"We built this bank for you," was one of 1st Mariner's earliest slogans. And there was no mistaking who the "you" was. Ordinary folks frustrated by the indifference their bank showed whenever they had a problem and really needed cash—that was 1st Mariner's target demographic.

The indefatigable new chairman oversaw seemingly every detail of the bank's start-up, including coming up with the corporate name.

He had always loved the water, and at first he toyed with names such as Fort McHenry Bank and Tidewater Bank, until he realized the latter had already been taken.

What he *didn't* want was a name with "Baltimore" in it. Years earlier, Bank of Baltimore officials had noted a reluctance among customers at their branches in Washington, D.C., Montgomery County and Northern Virginia to fully embrace the bank because of the parochial differences associated with the word "Baltimore" in the name.

Hale was not about to make the same mistake twice.

Finally he settled on 1st Mariner Bank. It had a nice ring to it. It was simple, yet classy. It had a nautical theme, but didn't beat you over the head with it, like a cheap seafood restaurant.

Not only that, Hale thought, but "it was generic enough that it could sell even in Cedar Rapids, Iowa. They're on the Mississippi River and they consider themselves to be mariners as much as the people in New Bedford, Mass."

Next he designed the logo, a golden compass similar to one he'd once had on the decals of his trucks. His love for tennis prompted him to consider Wimbledon colors, dark blue and dark green, for the bank's signage, business cards and brochures. He was friends with tennis great Pam Shriver and had her send over one of her Wimbledon jerseys so he could match the colors perfectly.

In typical Ed Hale fashion, he did not settle meekly into his new role as chairman, either.

He had bought the bank from 63-year-old J. Clarence Jameson III, founder of a Towson accounting firm, and George H. Mantakos, 52, a respected executive who had worked at two previous banks. But Jameson was summarily dismissed as chairman for having what Hale perceived to be an obstructionist attitude, and for making changes in the original deal that Hale resented.

Before Jameson had hit the bank of elevators to leave the building, Hale was knocking on the office door of Mantakos, the bank president.

"I just fired your buddy Jameson," Hale announced. "And as soon as I find out what you do, I'm going to fire you, too."

"Oh, he *hated* me for a while," Mantakos recalled. "I could tell in his eyes. We didn't get along at all."

The two settled into an uneasy co-existence for many months, until the veteran banker gradually won Hale's respect with his grasp of the intricacies of the business. Eventually they became good friends, to the point where at a retirement party for Mantakos, Hale stared at him and cracked: "I never *did* find out what you did."

Under Hale's direction, 1st Mariner quickly found its footing. Within four years, it had grown to 24 branches and $600 million in assets while employing some 450 people. Hale also wasted no time in becoming the public face of the institution, starring in a series of folksy commercials shot in his office in which he'd earnestly extol the endless virtues of hometown banking.

Things were going so well that the new chairman could afford to be cavalier when the bank found itself embroiled in a mini-controversy over its new slogan: "We treat you like a neighbor, not a number."

Officials at two other banks promptly got themselves in a lather over the catchphrase. They wrote to Hale, insisting it had originated with their banks and asking 1st Mariner to cease and desist from using it.

Hale responded by firing off a letter of his own—with tongue firmly in cheek—to the offended parties.

"Dear Sirs," it read. "Enclosed find respective copies of your letter concerning 1st Mariner Bank's advertising program. It seems that there is a dispute about the originality of the 'neighbor not a number' slogan.

"I submit that you two companies should arm-wrestle for the privilege of continued usage," the letter continued. "Let me know who the winner is and I'll take you on."

The slogan uproar became the lead item in a column by the *Sun's* Dan Rodricks, adding to Hale's growing reputation as a maverick banker thumbing his nose at the stuffy fat cats who still ruled the industry.

Hale was changing perceptions with the way he ran the bank, too, with a bottom-line focus and greater accountability expected from his employees.

Alex Hart, an analyst with Ferris Baker Watts, told the *Sun* that Hale "brought a businessman's perspective to running a bank, which is a more proactive and decisive management style."

It was a style that had served him well in his trucking and barge businesses. For old-school bankers like George Mantakos, however, the change was jarring.

With Ed Hale, Mantakos said, "there was never such a thing as bankers' hours. Ed could call you at 12 at night if he wanted to—or

1 in the morning, or whenever he (was) up writing all those notes—
with a question. And that's something the chairman of your old bank
would have never thought of doing.

"And he would schedule meetings at 7 or 8 in the morning, or a
dinner meeting at 9 at night. Ed sort of works 24/7 and he expected
some (employees) to do the same thing. But they had families and
Ed didn't. *This* was his family.

"I don't know if Ed ever slept," Mantakos continued with a
chuckle. "He would wake up in the morning with a pad of notes
and come (to the bank) and start in: 'This is what we're gonna do.'
And Joe and I would explain why we couldn't do it that fast and he'd
throw us out of his office.

"And ultimately he'd think about it for a while... and come back
and say: 'You know, what I was thinking about might not work.'"

Hale was dead serious about 1st Mariner Bank ingratiating itself
into the community, however. It became his over-riding focus. He
began holding breakfast meetings with customers, a practice he had
first started when he ran the Bank of Baltimore.

Coffee, doughnuts and pastries would be served. Hale and other
bank officials would be there to hear customer concerns. Mortgage
officers would be on hand for anyone interested in taking out a loan.

"It was the only bank I've ever seen do that," Mantakos said. "It
was a very good way to reach into the community.... People enjoyed
it. I enjoyed it. It was another way of proving 'We're here for you.' It
wasn't just a phrase."

There were a few missteps along the way. Perhaps the biggest was
a decision to put bank branches in seven Mars supermarkets. Within
two years, it was clear the branches were under-performing and they
were soon closed.

But by 2003, 1st Mariner had a robust $1 billion in assets and
750 employees, making it the third largest Baltimore-based bank.

To devote his full attention to his new venture, and because he had a fiduciary responsibility to his customers as a soon-to-be public company chair and CEO, Hale sold his still-lucrative trucking and barge businesses.

He also unloaded his ailing Peterbilt truck dealership, the only business he ever lost money on. Hale blamed incompetent management, led by a Philadelphian named Ed Brown, for the dealership's demise.

Hale had been desperate to wring every dollar he could out of the dying franchise, which he'd bought in 1998. When Canadian businessman John Arnscott expressed interest in buying it, the two men went head-to-head in series of bitter negotiating sessions, with Hale finally extracting more than he could have hoped for in the deal.

Years later, Arnscott would still wince when he recalled the back-and-forth between the two, famously adding to Hale's legacy with the line: "If I had an 800-lb. gorilla sitting on Ed and a .45 at his head, he'd still be telling me he'd kick my ass."

By now, though, it was Ed Hale who was in many ways the King Kong of his realm.

As the chairman of a hugely-successful bank that he'd started from scratch, he had grudgingly earned the respect of the downtown business establishment he purported to disdain. Between his salary (over $500,000 annually), bank stock (a reported $22 million in 2003) and real estate holdings, he was wealthy beyond his wildest dreams.

And as the star of 1st Mariner's ubiquitous TV commercials, he was also a genuine celebrity, recognized now wherever he went in Baltimore.

But some things didn't change—including his difficult relationship with his father.

One day, soon after the release of his sixth 1st Mariner commercial, Hale dropped by his parents' house for lunch. He was on his way to buy the vacant Thompson Steel Co. plant off North

Point Road, where he hoped to move his trucking and warehouse operations and create jobs near his old neighborhood.

"I show up and my father's sitting there watching CNN," he recalled. "He doesn't even acknowledge me coming in the house."

Hale happened to have a copy of the new commercial with him. After lunch, he popped it into the cassette recorder for his parents to see.

Years earlier, Hale had been nervous and self-conscious when he first started shooting the 1st Mariner spots. But gradually he'd become more polished and confident in his delivery, able to look squarely into the camera and deliver his lines with an earnestness that seemed to emanate from his very soul.

Now he was proud of how this new commercial had turned out, and eager to see his parents' reaction.

When the commercial finished playing, Carol Hale gushed: "Boy, Eddie, you're really getting pretty good at this! You're really believable!"

No such praise emanated from his father, however.

"Without looking up," Hale recalled, "he says: 'You know, your right eye is bigger than your left eye.'"

Long resigned to not getting approval and encouragement from his father, Hale shrugged and thought: "Whatever."

Nevertheless, the powerful bank chairman, who'd been on top of the world a few minutes earlier, left the house shortly after in a far less triumphant mood. His relationship with his father would remain difficult until the elder Hale's death in 2002.

# CHAPTER 15

## Working Hard, Playing Hard

Even at the very height of his success, juggling the responsibilities of running a bank, a trucking firm and a barge company and putting in ridiculous hours, Ed Hale resisted being called a workaholic.

"Business is a hobby with me," he'd tell everyone. "It's probably my favorite thing to do."

Why didn't people *get* that? he wondered.

Couldn't they see the unbridled joy he took from all the wheeling and dealing, from the endless quest to be the biggest and the best at what he did? Even if he had to take gut-churning personal and financial risks along the way?

"Ed had demonstrated—and to this day (still does)—the incredible will that he can get himself into any difficulty and get himself out of it," says his old friend Buzzy Krongard. "But it doesn't always work. And Ed was balancing a lot of balls.

"There are some people, that's their life," Krongard continued. "They just kind of enjoy it in a strange way. Jimmy the Greek said the next best thing to winning is losing. It's action that counts. I mean, that's Ed. Trying to talk Ed out of doing something, you may as well save your breath."

Which didn't mean there weren't times when Hale's head felt ready to explode from all the stress. And at those times, he'd invariably turn to the other passions in his life: tennis, hunting and fishing.

Hale had loved tennis since his Camp Najerog days, and now it became a favorite way to blow off steam and use his competitive nature to full advantage.

After a desultory career on the Sparrow's Point High tennis team—not one win, not even a *set*—Hale had single-mindedly dedicated himself to improving his game. And not just improving it—excelling at it, too.

He became so accomplished that he played both singles and doubles at Essex Community College without losing a match. He won the base championship while in the Air Force. And a few years later, when his play began to attract attention around Baltimore and he was invited to join the prestigious Homeland Racquet Club in 1969, he leaped at the chance.

Most of the matches were played on clay courts. The competition was fierce, the level of play extremely high. Former college players and a smattering of grizzled vets who'd spent time on the pro circuit populated the league, which included teams from area clubs like Elkridge, L'Hirondelle, Suburban and St. Timothy's.

With his big overhead, eye-hand coordination and an innate feel for the game, Hale made the A team in short order. He quickly developed a reputation as a dogged player who would run down every point, even if it killed him.

"He had a very good game," recalled George Duncan, an ophthalmologist who played on the Homeland team for many years. "But his strength was his competitiveness. He could achieve beyond his level of experience.... It was probably the way he approached everything in life."

Those who played with him marveled at his focus—how he could leap out of the car after a long day, grab his racquet and instantly have his head in the game, no matter what fresh horror he'd been dealing with at the office.

"I beat him once," says long-time friend John Buren, a former WJZ-TV sports anchor and current Long & Foster Realtor who played countless matches against Hale. "Beat him on hard court. At Bare Hills (Racquet and Fitness Club.). But on clay court, if God were to give him a healthy shoulder now and he hadn't played in two years… he'd beat me.

"Just 'cause he *has* to. 'Cause he's little Eddie Hale from the wrong side of the tracks and '*Goddammit, I'm going to show you!*'"

At Camp Najerog, tennis had given the rough-and-tumble kid from Sparrow's Point the confidence to compete with the rich kids. Now the game helped give the young boot-strapping businessman entrée into a world he had only dreamed of.

Now he was playing with hugely-successful Jewish businessmen, as well as with doctors, lawyers and accountants, among others. Over beers after matches, or at weekend cookouts at the opulent homes of well-heeled members, the talk would often turn to business. Hale would eagerly tune in.

"They'd talk about real estate deals, bank deals, all sorts of stuff, and I would sit there and soak up all this knowledge," he would say years later. "It helped me in business. It made me more confident that I could talk to and hang out with anyone."

But there were awkward moments with the tennis crowd, too—even as Hale's personal wealth and prominence in the community grew.

At one point, he was black-balled for membership at the ritzy L'Hirondelle, the oldest private social club in Baltimore. Later, he heard it was partly because some members feared he might bring black Blast players to the club.

"I don't want to join a club that would have me as a member," he joked to friends, dusting off a variation of the old Groucho Marx line even as he was deeply offended by the snub.

At other times, he could feel some of the players and their wives studying him, unsure of what to make of the pugnacious trucker with the rough edges in their midst.

"I was a curiosity: the guy from Dundalk," he remembered.

He even recalled one snooty Elkridge member going so far as to bring up his pedigree in a face-to-face conversation and sniff: "You could *never* be a member of this club."

Hale extracted a small measure of retribution the next time he played there. With the snobby woman watching, he pretended to scratch his butt, then blew his nose and sprayed mucus on the court in the middle of a match.

At age 57, though, with three shoulder surgeries behind him, he hung up his racquet for good. From then on, it was fishing and hunting geese and duck on his Talbot County farm that helped Ed Hale unwind.

Fishing had always been his first love, ever since he first dropped a hook in the smelly, murky waters off the Point as a boy. Now, as the demands of his businesses grew, he began taking trips to Canada, looking for ever-more-isolated places that offered the opportunity to reel in trophy fish and decompress.

In the early 90's, he found his fishing Taj Mahal at Hatchet Lake, a remote lake in northeastern Saskatchewan teeming with northern pike, trout, Canadian walleye and arctic grayling.

For a man looking for peace and quiet, it was dead solid perfect.

Hatchet Lake Lodge, situated on an island in the middle of the lake, catered to well-heeled customers and was reachable only by aircraft. There were no TV's or phones in the cabins. There was no cell phone or Internet service.

There were only miles and miles of clear blue water teeming with fish, ringed by majestic pine trees as far as the eye could see.

It was one of the most breath-taking settings Hale had ever seen.

"The second-best feeling in the world," he'd say, assuming you weren't too dense to realize what the best feeling was, "is sitting in a boat near the Arctic Circle and your native Cree guide shuts that motor off and you look around and go: '*Whoa!*'

"It's such a pristine environment. There's no trash in the water. No noise. No lights. No airplanes."

Hale would also become fast friends with Harvey Kroll, the lodge's irreverent general manager, who had attended an all-boys Catholic school in Saskatchewan and played in a rock band called Pontius Pilate and the Nail-Drivers.

But the two did not exactly hit it off the first time Hale set foot in the place.

"I thought: boy, this guy's going to be a real prick," Kroll recalls with a laugh now. "He had that way about him."

But that perception changed when Kroll received a phone call and had to deliver terrible news to the Baltimore businessman: Hale's niece had been killed in a car accident.

Kroll accompanied Hale on the plane ride back to Saskatoon, so he could catch a connecting flight home for the funeral. The two talked the whole time and Kroll discovered another side to the macho, tough-talking Hale.

"That changed everything," Kroll says. "I saw how deeply rooted he was to his family."

The two became close, finding they shared the same ribald sense of humor and off-kilter view of the world. Kroll grew to respect Hale so much that when he had an opportunity to buy the lodge a few years ago, he sought the Baltimore business mogul's advice before closing the deal.

Now, after 21 years of visits, Hale has achieved celebrity status at Hatchet Lake.

"When Ed's coming to the lodge," Kroll says, "I alert most of my staff. They call him Uncle Eddie. They know it's going to be a fun four days."

Indeed, when Hale and his party descend on Hatchet Lake, the place takes on a raucous frat house atmosphere. Two years ago, in fact, Hale was the chief culprit in a tit-for-tat prank that has already achieved legendary status.

Arriving with Blast coach Danny Kelly and two other friends, Brian Kavanaugh and Alex Van Ettan, Hale promptly went into full prank-pulling mode. He arranged to have someone at the lodge tell Van Ettan that there was a problem with his bill and that his credit card had been rejected.

Not only that, the lodge rep told Van Ettan, but payment in full was required immediately. Otherwise, his butt would have to be on the first plane back to Saskatoon.

Van Ettan was properly confused and mortified. He sputtered that he had paid Hale beforehand for the trip, to which Hale replied with a straight face: "I don't know what you're talking about."

They let Van Ettan twist in the wind for several minutes, until finally letting him in on the joke. Immediately, he began plotting his revenge.

"I'm going to get that motherfucker," he muttered to Kelly and Kavanaugh.

And the plan he came up with was a doozey.

Quickly, he arranged for a guide to lock one of the camp's huge Husky dogs in the bathroom of Hale's cabin when the group was out fishing. When Hale returned that afternoon, undressed and opened the bathroom door to take a shower, the frightened dog shot out between his legs, practically dismembering him and provoking a heart attack.

A tremulous lodge worker soon ratted out Van Ettan.

Now it was Hale who plotted his pay-back.

Again, he enlisted the help of Kroll, which did not take a lot of arm-twisting. Harvey Kroll loved this sort of thing.

Once, during his senior year at the Saskatchewan Catholic high school, Kroll had snuck into one of the darkened church confessionals. Pretending to be a priest, he had heard confessions from his classmates for 20 minutes until the real priest showed up and busted him.

Kroll had nearly been expelled for the stunt. But that had hardly dampened his enthusiasm for creative mayhem of the sort Hale was planning.

Now, Hale had two lodge workers wrap his arm in a bandage and smear it with red food coloring to make it look like blood.

Kroll handed him a beer. Then Hale marched down to Van Ettan's cabin, where Kelly and Kavanaugh had also gathered. Hale pretended to be both seriously hurt and outraged.

By all accounts, he delivered an Academy Award-winning performance.

"This is unbelievable!" he sputtered to his friends. "I just got mauled by this dog and fucking Harvey hands me a beer and tells me to suck it up! That's it, we're never coming back here again!"

The three others were skeptical about Hale's story. But an hour later, when the four were at dinner and others were staring at a wincing Hale and wondering what sort of catastrophe had caused his bloodied arm, a worried-looking Kroll approached their table.

"OK, Ed," he said with a straight face, "we're going to fly you out by seaplane to a native settlement. They have a clinic there. Hopefully they can stitch you up. I'm real sorry this happened."

The hook was in. Now the others were convinced of Hale's wounds. So convinced, in fact, that Van Ettan insisted on accompanying Hale and paying for the emergency flight.

But Kroll explained the tiny seaplane could hold only one other person beside the pilot.

"We'll settle up later," he told Van Ettan.

Then he walked Hale, groaning in pain now, in the direction of the dock. The others watched morosely, figuring their fishing trip was now officially ruined, until Hale and Kroll were out of sight. The three friends couldn't see the seaplane, but they could hear the pilot revving the engine. This was followed by a roar that sounded like the plane taking off.

Seconds later, Hale burst into the dining room sans the bloody bandages, shooting his shocked buddies the bird and cackling triumphantly.

"He got them good," Kroll says, still laughing at the memory. "The looks on their faces . . ."

In keeping with the raucous jokes and sophomoric hijinks that characterize most Ed Hale fishing trips, his infamous fart machine has made many memorable appearances at Hatchet Lake.

Jim Lighthizer, the former Maryland transportation secretary and Anne Arundel County executive, recalled one particular time he and Hale teamed up to use the machine on their stoic Cree fishing guide as the three of them sat in a boat fishing.

In the morning, Hale carried the transmitter. Every few minutes, he would press the button and the sound of a loud, ungodly-long fart would pierce the lake's near-sacred stillness.

"Hale, you're a pig!" Lighthizer admonished his friend each time. "You're just swine! God dammit, you're an *animal!* What did you eat?"

Each time Hale apologized profusely and went back to fishing. And each time, the guide said nothing.

After lunch, when the three went out on the lake again, it was Lighthizer who carried the transmitter.

Now it was the former politician who seemed plagued by epic bouts of flatulence every few minutes, sheepishly murmuring "Excuse me!" as Hale berated him for his crudeness. ("Jim, you bastard, can't you *control* yourself?")

Again, the guide showed no reaction.

Hale and Lighthizer began to fear the man was deaf.

Finally, though, after another hour's worth of this torture, the guide couldn't take it anymore.

"Jesus, you white guys are *sick*! I thought Barry Switzer was bad!" he cried, referring to the legendary former football coach of Oklahoma and the Dallas Cowboys who had visited the lodge. "But I've never seen anybody with gas like you guys have!"

For sheer gross-out impact, however, you'd have to go some to beat the stunt Hale pulled in 2007, when he brought the fart machine and a bucket of water into a bathroom located adjacent to the lodge's bar and a massage area.

As patrons enjoyed cocktails before dinner and soft mood music and the smell of scented candles wafted from the massage area, Hale went into his act.

"Oh, God! Oh, no! Oh, God, no!" he began wailing, alternately hitting the fart machine and pouring water in the toilet to simulate an explosive bout of diarrhea.

When he finally emerged from the bathroom after some 10 minutes of this, the bar customers were engulfed with laughter. And a grinning masseuse emerged from the massage area to announce: "You know, I think I ought to have a word with the chef."

Even when Hale and his party aren't at Hatchet Lake, the byplay between Hale and Kroll never ceases.

A few years ago, a letter from a Mr. Colt Connelly of the Connelly Funeral Home in Dundalk arrived at the lodge.

"Dear Mr. Kroll," it began, "Mr. Hale has called to instruct me on what to do in the event of his death. He would like to have his mortal remains frozen and sent to Hatchet Lake, where he would like to have a Viking funeral performed complete with a wooden boat or canoe with flaming arrows shot into it.

"I hope that you complete your end of this arrangement when Mr. Hale's remains eventually arrive at Hatchet Lake. At (that) point, my firm is washing its hands of the matter, because we want no part of this."

Kroll responded by calling a florist in Baltimore and having a nice funeral bouquet sent to Hale's home, as a prelude to the glorious day in which he could fulfill his buddy's wishes and send him off to Valhalla in proper style.

# CHAPTER 16

## A Tower Rises From the Wasteland

Ed Hale was still dreaming big—bigger than ever, many said—as the New Millennium unfolded.

In the spring of 2001, he announced a grand plan to build a $1 billion complex that included an office tower, condominiums, restaurants, retail stores, a hotel and a 244-slip marina on a desolate stretch of Canton's industrial waterfront that looked like the setting for the Mel Gibson "Mad Max" movies.

Rusting oil tanks, rotting piers, rebar jutting from the earth like bony skeletal fingers and acres of toxic waste were just some of the delights awaiting the contractor brave enough to don a hazmat suit and tackle the job at Boston and Clinton streets

Everyone told Hale he was crazy.

When he added that he planned to put $41 million of his own cash into the deal, the critics practically fitted him for a straitjacket.

"Very early on, when I was mayor, we had a press conference down there," Martin O'Malley recalled. "We had Mikulski, we had (Rep. Elijah E.) Cummings, we had (Maryland junior Sen. Ben) Cardin, we had a number of elected officials for a ground-breaking declaration of intent... to redevelop the brownfields.

"It was tumbleweeds and toxins, a miserable place. I vaguely recall someone saying to me—I don't recall which member of Congress it was: 'Martin, none of this is going to happen in your lifetime. But it's great that we started.'"

But Hale was far from insane, as his critics would have it. The gentrification of Canton was well underway and he could envision the need for office space and all the amenities that would be offered in the complex he planned to develop.

The area was becoming a residential hot spot for droves of young people: yuppies and hipsters and disaffected families tired of the soulless suburbs and intrigued by the glittering waterfront renovation going on in such places as Locust Point and Federal Hill, the Inner Harbor, Harbor East and Fells Point.

Easy access to nearby I-95 was a huge draw. Real estate prices were soaring. Homes were selling for $350,000 and more.

Against all odds, gritty old Canton, an after-thought in the minds of many Baltimoreans, was becoming *hip*.

And Ed Hale was as amazed as anyone at the transformation.

"I used to say that if God were going to give an enema to the state of Maryland, He would do it right here in Canton," Hale recalled. "It was that ugly."

But the market was there now and he was ready to take full advantage of it. Moreover, he was convinced the proposed complex would greatly benefit the eastern part of the city and make it an even more desirable place to live.

"There's not even a place around here to buy towels," one woman had complained bitterly to Hale weeks earlier.

*Towels?*

Oh, Hale would give them a place to buy towels—and whatever else they wanted, too.

The new complex, he told reporters, would be called Canton Crossing. It was a name he came up with after hearing the 1982

Crosby, Stills and Nash tune "Southern Cross," about a man who sails the world after a doomed love affair.

And rising in its midst like a giant monolith would be the complex's centerpiece: a 17-story, 480,000-square foot office tower that would house dozens of area businesses and serve as the headquarters for 1st Mariner Bank, the Blast and Hale's trucking and shipping concerns.

The tower would also feature a dozen penthouse condominiums, one of which he planned to make his new home. He was living right down the road in the ritzy 14-floor Anchorage Tower building and never tired of looking out at the water and Baltimore skyline, which he ranked as one of the most magnificent in the world behind Hong Kong, San Francisco and New York.

Now, from his new digs at the top of the office tower, he would have an even more breath-taking, panoramic view of the iconic neon Domino Sugar sign, the entire Baltimore harbor, the stadiums and skyscrapers of downtown and all the quirky neighborhoods in-between.

But before ground could be broken, Ed Hale had to settle a simmering turf war.

One which started over salt, of all things.

As it happened, Hale's offices at 1801 S. Clinton Street were adjacent to Rukert Terminals Corp., a shipping company owned by his brother-in-law, Norm Rukert. Rukert had huge piles of de-icing salt on its property for its trucks. And the salt was blowing onto the cars of 1st Mariner employees, creating a morale problem for the bank's chairman.

"People were complaining their cars were getting pitted by the salt piles," Hale said. "Norm wouldn't cover them. He said 'We were here first.'"

An attorney for Rukert finally hit on a solution: how about if the two warring sides swapped land?

Rukert would trade its 18 acres, which were closer to Canton's housing and retail district and the increased visibility of the Boston Street corner, for Hale's more remote 28 acres. And Rukert would pay Hale a sum of money for the larger parcel of land.

"Sounds good to me," Hale told them. "Pay me $5 million and we have a deal."

Hearing this, the Rukert people nearly spit their coffee across the room.

"That's crazy," they answered. "You're insane."

Originally, Hale told friends, he would have swapped the land even-up. But now he was looking to cut the best deal possible, even if it involved playing hard-ball with a family member.

"We'll pay you $2 million," the Rukert people counter-offered.

"That's an insult," Hale replied. "Don't even talk to me."

Soon the president of the shipping company, George F. ("Bud") Nixon Jr., was back for one last negotiating session. Hale had George Mantakos sit in on this one.

"Bud Nixon wags a finger," Hale recalled, "and says 'This is our final offer. If you don't take this, we're going to walk.'"

Hale figured Nixon was about to offer something in the neighborhood of $2.3 million, which he would have gladly taken. But when Nixon opened his mouth, it was Hale's turn to nearly keel over. The final Rukert offer was $4.8 million.

"I'll think about it," Hale told Nixon.

He tried to keep his features flat and his voice calm. But inside, Hale remembered, "I'm like Daffy Duck doing back-flips around the room and going 'WOO! WOO! WOO!'"

When Nixon left, Mantakos looked at Hale in disbelief and said: "How did you keep a straight face?"

There was still much work to be done before the grand project Hale envisioned was shovel-ready.

Other regulatory hurdles had to be cleared. Hale had to get

the zoning classification changed from industrial to Planned Urban Development (PUD), to accommodate residential and non-residential buildings. And he began the task of cleaning up the oil on the property, where a former Exxon refinery had been located.

With each step, though, the howling of the skeptics seemed to grow ever louder.

One day, Hale and George Mantakos met with a man named Mark Deering and other brokers of MacKenzie Commercial Real Estate Services in Towson.

Hale hoped to hire the company to rent office space in the new tower. He spoke excitedly about the project for a few minutes and showed Deering a rendering of what the new building would look like: a massive octagon with a distinctive green hip roof and red brick façade jutting toward the heavens over Canton.

When Hale was finished, Deering appeared less than impressed.

"Instead of saying 'Oh, boy, thank you for coming!' or 'Oh, boy, this is a great opportunity for us!'" Hale recalled, "he said 'That's the hinterlands. No one will ever go there.'"

Hale was stunned. And livid. Without another word, he closed his portfolio and walked out.

"Ed just got up and left the room!" Mantakos says with wonder in his voice all these years later. "And I'm just sitting there! I'm waiting for him to turn the lights out! I'm serious! He had that look in his eye.

"I (thought): That sucker's gonna turn the lights out! I *know* he is! Then I just got up and left with him."

He laughs dryly. "It wasn't a long meeting."

Hale encountered more doubters when he submitted plans for the new tower to the city's Urban Design and Architecture Review Panel (UDARP.)

A short while later, one of Hale's engineers reported back on the panel's findings. What followed was an exchange worthy of an Abbot

& Costello routine.

"They say the windows are too violent," the engineer told Hale.

"Too violet?" Hale said.

"No, *violent*," the engineer replied.

Hale was incredulous.

"Are you fucking with me?" Hale asked. "The windows are too *violent?*"

"Right. That's what they said. Violent."

"What does that even mean?" Hale wanted to know. But the engineer had no answer. Neither, it seemed, did anyone else.

Steaming now and convinced he was a victim of needless bureaucratic wrangling and red-tape, Hale picked up the phone and called Martin O'Malley.

Quickly, he filled in the mayor on the UDARP finding, which immediately devolved into another comedy sketch.

"They say the windows are too violent," Hale told the mayor.

"Too *violent?*" O'Malley said. "What does that mean?"

"I don't know," Hale replied.

O'Malley wondered aloud if perhaps the panel meant the windows were too *velvet*, instead of too violent or too violet.

But by now Hale was at the end of his rope.

"I need you to step in and stop the madness," he said.

The rest of the conversation is lost to history, although O'Malley, now Maryland's governor, laughingly recalls: "He basically said 'I'm building the goddamn tower. Instead of giving me shit, they should be giving me a medal.'"

Eventually, the windows were approved and the project moved ahead until late the following year, when Hale came up against another problem—a *major* problem.

This one was rather stout and wore a house-dress.

And she spoke in a Bawlmer accent thicker than cream of crab soup.

# CHAPTER 17

## The Saga of Girlie Hoffman

Lula Elizabeth "Girlie" Hoffman was 84 and had the misfortune—
if that was the word— of residing at 1517 S. Clinton Street in the
year 2003.

She had been born in the two-story row house in 1918 and had
lived there all her life. Until 1999, part of the house had served as
Hoffman's Bar, a family-run saloon that catered to truckers, sailors
and longshoremen looking for a cold beer and a hamburger.

"It was a real old-time bar," Ken Jones would recall. "Dirty, dingy,
with a lot of knotty pine that went back to the 50's look."

Girlie had grown up in the once-bustling industrial
neighborhood with seven sisters and three brothers. Now she lived
by herself, although she had once owned a monkey named Dinky
that, according to legend, would swill Budweiser and masturbate
copiously in front of the customers when it got hammered.

The monkey was no longer a problem. Girlie had reportedly
given it the heave-ho when it began biting her.

But this *was* a problem: Girlie's home was smack-dab in the
way of the tower and mega-complex Ed Hale was developing on
this forlorn strip of Canton. And while the old gal was stubbornly

refusing any and all entreaties for her to leave, she was also terrified that the powerful businessman and his lawyers would find a way to force her out.

There was no question that they wanted her gone. But by January of 2003, negotiations to buy her out had been largely unsuccessful, even though Hale had offered Girlie up to $225,000 for the ramshackle property.

This, his lawyer, Stanley Fine had assured everyone, was "a very generous and fair offer." Especially considering that the assessed value of the house was $47,900.

Fine was telling reporters that a possible next move would be to ask the city to condemn the property and sell the 20-by-95-foot lot back to Hale. But Hale realized what a PR disaster that would be for 1st Mariner if the media ever got hold of the story—and how bad it would be for the bank's business.

"Also, it wasn't in my nature to do something like that," Hale says now. "Foreclose on an old lady hanging on in a place like that? Uh-uh."

Meanwhile, Girlie had been the subject of a sympathetic front-page story in the *Sun*, which read as if it should have carried the headline: "PITILESS DEVELOPER CACKLES AS POOR OLD LADY WITH HEART CONDITION IS ROUSTED FROM ANCESTRAL HOME."

"She would call the Sunpapers all the time," Hale recalled, "trying to make me look like the white devil slave-master."

For an old East Baltimore girl whose life was spent largely running a dusty bar stuck in a time warp—beers for a buck! Noodle soup for $1.25!—Girlie Hoffman knew how to spin a story.

"He's been there not even a year," Girlie was quoted as saying of Hale in the *Sun* article. "He wants to take my home, me being here 84 years."

Much of the article consisted of Girlie's wistful reminiscences of her family and the bar-keep life, including the time she met Gene Hackman and Will Smith when they shot a scene for the movie "Enemy of the State" inside Hoffman's.

For that, Girlie reported, she was paid the princely sum of $3,000 and marveled at the sumptuous catered meals prepared for the cast and crew.

It was only toward the end of the article that Girlie's negotiating strategy with Ed Hale was revealed: she had originally planned to ask the tower developer for a cool $1 million to vacate the premises.

But when she'd mentioned that figure to her lawyer and he'd choked on his morning doughnut, she'd lowered the price to a more accommodating $500,000.

Only on further advice from legal counsel had she dropped the price to $225,000. Then, having second thoughts about leaving, she'd pulled the offer from the table altogether.

So the stalemate continued. And the negotiations between Hale and Girlie Hoffman—already six months old—went on for nearly six more months.

As work crews continued to swarm over Hale's property, remediating the oil-soaked ground, his lieutenants took it upon themselves to try other forms of persuasion on Girlie.

"I would even bring in crews at night that would work around her house," Ken Jones said. "They'd be breaking concrete around the clock to disturb the living crap out of her and convince her to move."

Finally, in mid-summer, a deal was struck. Girlie Hoffman agreed to sell her house to Hale for $266,600. And he agreed to pay her monthly food and housing expenses for as long as she lived.

In another front-page *Sun* article announcing the settlement and the old woman's bittersweet feelings about moving out—this time it was noted that she'd had her mother laid out on Hoffman's bar after her death, respectfully screened off from the liquor bottles by a white sheet —Girlie's attitude toward Hale had changed markedly.

"He is a very nice man, ain't he?" she was quoted as saying of the banking mogul.

The article went on to report that Hale had graciously given Girlie "plenty of time to pack up and sell off choice artifacts, such as a floor-length spittoon trough and 1940's-era wooden bar well worn by thousands of bent elbows."

By the fall, Girlie Hoffman had moved to Dundalk to live with her sister-in-law, Marie Hoffman. And Girlie's old house, with all its musty memories and the raucous laughter of thousands of waterfront denizens still echoing off its barroom walls, succumbed to the wrecking ball in late December.

But far from being depressed, Girlie seemed positively chipper when she spoke to the *Sun* the day before the demolition.

"I got it so good, I don't think nothing of it," she said. "Here, I got it lovely. That's why I don't miss being away from it."

The old wooden bar and dozens of signs, knick-knacks and artifacts were bought by a woman named Denise Whiting, owner of the Hampden restaurant Café Hon, who planned to use them in a new saloon she was opening.

Ed Hale contracted with a job-training non-profit called Second Chance to haul the rest of the stuff away and sell it in their warehouse, earning himself a tax deduction in the process.

As for the giant spittoon that had once been used as a urinal by those patrons too inebriated to make it to the men's room, no one seemed quite sure where it ended up.

The builders of 1st Mariner Tower were now free to proceed with construction. And Ed Hale would go on to pay the old woman $275 a month for the next six years, for a total of $19,800.

In a fitting post-script, Girlie Hoffman attended church services with Ed Hale's mother, Carol Hale, until the crusty former bar owner died in 2009.

# CHAPTER 18

## Living on Top of the World

Construction on the shiny new 1st Mariner Bank office tower was completed in 2006. Six months later, a lone tenant took up residence in the building's only apartment, a 10,000-square-foot penthouse that seemed to touch the clouds and was lavish enough to shame an oil sheik.

Everything about Ed Hale's new place was eye-popping.

There were 14-foot coffered ceilings and marble wainscoting throughout. A polished Steinway grand piano and an enormous fireplace dominated the living room. An airy art gallery filled with expensive paintings and sculptures was located just off the main entrance.

The gleaming kitchen, with a barrel ceiling, cost $350,000 to out-fit and was voted "Kitchen of the Year" in *Kitchen and Bathroom* magazine. There were almost more Oriental rugs scattered about than existed in the entire Orient.

The doors were solid mahogany, each seemingly thick enough to withstand an assault with a battle axe.

Even the elevators were the fastest and most efficient in existence; a ride to the top floors felt as if one were being whisked silently to another part of the cosmos.

Total costs of installing Hale in what was probably the grandest new waterfront address in Baltimore: a cool $2,005,066.

"The whole thing," he admitted years later, "was just way over the top."

As he had with everything else in his life, Ed Hale had worked hard to ensure that the tower would be a success from the very beginning.

Even before the first shovel broke ground, he was lobbying businesses from all over Maryland to relocate their offices to 1501 S. Clinton Street and the distinctive new building with the green hip roof that would be seen for miles in any direction.

As it happened, not only were companies willing to come to the Canton "hinterlands," they were eager to do so, lured by the prospect of installing their workers in a brand new building with 30,000-square feet of office space on each floor, ample parking, jaw-dropping views of the harbor and a growing sense that this was now a hot place to do business.

1st Mariner's operations took up three floors of the tower. But the building quickly reached an occupancy rate of over 90-per cent as well-known companies such as Carefirst, About Faces Day Spa and Salon, aerospace and defense contractor Alliant Techsystems, Inc., and the Baltimore-area engineering firm of Whitney, Bailey, Cox & Magnani, as well, as a Johns Hopkins Hospital outpatient clinic, filled the place.

Still, the critics took their shots at the tower—especially that first year.

One memorable blog post called it "Ed Hale's phallic symbol." Another accused of him of "uglying-up" Canton with this new "monstrosity," as if the former bleak stretch of industrial wasteland had been a veritable Garden of Eden beforehand.

But as he had when he went into banking, Hale paid little

attention to the nay-sayers. His regard for bloggers, already low, cratered even further. He viewed them as the stereotypical losers in Metallica T-shirts slouched with their laptops in their parents' basements, nursing long-simmering resentments and hurling invective into cyberspace to make themselves feel better.

The bitter blogger, Hale was convinced, was often "the person who's never done shit in his whole life."

In some ways, he viewed them as part of a larger segment of the population known as CAVE, or Citizens Against Virtually Everything, who would find something to carp about with a cure for cancer.

There was also this: Hale had always seen himself as a visionary. And he realized visionaries were often scorned at first, their grand ideas ridiculed. Galileo, DaVinci, Ben Franklin, Alexander Graham Bell, Henry Ford, Steve Jobs—had any of their initial pronouncements been greeted with sprinkled flower petals and hosannas?

Not that he was putting himself in the same league as those titans of innovation. But if the skeptics had savaged *them,* well, Ed Hale could live with the jeers and doubting, too.

Hale also remembered only too well the initial public relations drubbing that one of his mentors, Mayor William Donald Schaefer, had taken when he championed Harborplace as a transformational centerpiece for downtown Baltimore.

Hale was convinced the 1st Mariner tower and adjoining shopping complex would have a similar effect on the eastern part of the city. And it burned him that the braying dim-wits and knuckle-draggers now taking to their keyboards and attacking him on-line failed to see that.

Not that he was without his defenders, those who, early on, recognized what his efforts meant to the revitalization of a moribund strip of Canton.

"It was Ed's vision that put that whole thing on the table," said

James Kraft, the city councilman who represents Canton.

Kraft said when he first looked at Hale's plans for the massive tower and complex, "I thought it was pretty grandiose. But given all Ed had done, I thought he could pull it off."

For his part, Hale plunged eagerly into his new life in his sumptuous penthouse and enjoyed showing it off—at least at first.

A few days after moving in, he invited his mother over for her first look at the place. She brought along some 20 of the "church ladies" from Inverness Presbyterian in Dundalk, as well as Bob Dillard, the senior pastor.

After giving them the grand tour, which provoked the requisite oohing and ahhing, Hale announced: "Now, if you'll all accompany me, I want to show you a painting of my mother in her younger days. She really looked quite fetching."

Carol Hale, long used to her son's endless teasing and dumb jokes, merely rolled her eyes and thought: Now what?

The group dutifully accompanied Ed Hale to one of the spacious bathrooms. He snapped on the light and stepped aside.

There, hanging from one wall, was a large baroque oil painting of a pouting female musician in a flowing black garment, the top open to reveal her heaving breasts.

As the group exploded in laughter, Carol Hale could only shake her head and wonder: When is this going to end? I'm in my 80's. He's in his 60's. When does it *end?*

In the months that followed, Hale entertained often at the penthouse, reveling in the "wow factor" it elicited from his guests.

Ever the Democratic Party loyalist, he cheerfully held fundraisers for Senators Barbara Mikulski and Ben Cardin, as well as for Gov. Martin O'Malley, Rep. C.A. Dutch Ruppersberger and then-Baltimore-mayoral candidate Stephanie Rawlings-Blake, all of whom were thrilled to mingle with well-heeled donors in such an opulent setting.

The new place tended to impress the beautiful young women who visited, too.

Except... when these same women visited on certain evenings when other events were taking place in the apartment, well, things could get awkward.

Once, after a fund-raiser for O'Malley, the governor and a few other guests lingered later into the night, chatting and enjoying their surroundings and showing no signs of leaving.

This was quietly driving Hale crazy, since one of his dates was waiting for him in a nearby bedroom.

Tapping his foot impatiently, looking at the clock and pacing distractedly about the place, Hale did everything but fling the door open, whip an accusatory finger at the governor and his pals, and shout: "GET OUT!"

Finally, he could stand it no longer.

"Governor," he said, "with all due respect, I've got company. Would you guys please take a hike?"

Rising, O'Malley huffed jokingly: "Well. I've been thrown out of better places that this."

Then, gazing about once more, he added: "Come to think of it, no I haven't."

Within months, though, when the excitement of decorating and entertaining had worn off, Hale began having second thoughts about his new place.

At times, especially late at night, he resembled a Gatsby-esque figure, padding silently about his palatial abode high above the water with a growing feeling of discontent. At times, staring out at the darkness, he'd hear in his head the sultry voice of Peggy Lee singing her melancholy 1960's hit "Is That All There Is?"

"I distinctly remember sitting there one night and thinking: this is not me," he recalled of life in the penthouse. "I just didn't feel comfortable being there."

He still loved the magnificent view—he'd had the building angled specifically so that it afforded the best sight-lines of downtown Baltimore on one side and Fort McHenry on the other. And there were clear days when the clouds seemed to practically dance off the waves to dazzling effect, days when he was convinced there was no other sight quite like it anywhere else on earth.

But over time, it was clear to Hale that the place was simply too ritzy and gaudy for him. And too damn close to his office at the bank, which was located only one floor below.

"It would take me literally 27 seconds to go to work," he recalled. "And 27 seconds to go home."

There was no transition between the worlds of work and home, no morning commute during which he could strategize and gear up for the day ahead, no evening drive home during which to decompress after a stressful 10 or 12 hours.

"There were times," he said, "when there were four or five days in a row when I would never leave the building, it was so busy. It got to the point where I hated going there."

For an inherently private man, there was also little privacy. All guests had to check in with the security desk in the lobby. Which meant there were always people in the building who knew about the comings and goings of both Ed Hale and his guests—especially when those guests were occasional dates.

"At the end," Hale said, "I couldn't wait to get out.

Soon enough, events would conspire to force him from the penthouse even more quickly than he'd planned.

But in typical Ed Hale fashion, he would go out with a bang, not a whimper.

So it was that in January 2009, he threw a big party in the penthouse to celebrate the end of the dreaded 20 years of alimony payments to his first wife, Sheila Thacker.

It was a catered, stag-only affair, played strictly for laughs.

The guest list of some 200 included a veritable who's who of area politicians, power brokers and celebrities, along with friends and business connections Hale had known for years.

Hale had asked his old nemesis, Jim Smith, to show up with his judge's robes and gavel as part of the show. The former judge who had killed him in his divorce years earlier happily obliged, officially decreeing that Edwin Frank Hale was now free of the onerous burden of monster court-mandated payments to his ex, ending his long national nightmare.

One by one, speakers took the podium to roast the guest of honor. Resplendent in a navy-blue banker's suit, Ed Hale seemed relaxed, laughing at each good-natured dig and moldy anecdote from his past.

If there was a glitch in the proceedings, it came toward the end of the evening when Buzzy Krongard, his old friend, commandeered the microphone.

Krongard began reading from a lengthy poem he had written especially for the occasion:

*We gather here together*
*On this most auspicious night*
*To note the emancipation of this person on my right.*

*To do so I must bore you*
*With an ugly, sordid tale;*
*But that's the best description*
*Of Edwin Frank Hale.*

What followed were ever-more barbed remarks about everything from Hale's banking acumen and art collection to his dealings with politicos and his philandering ways.

Much of it was greeted with strained laughter or winces and cries of "Ouch!" But Krongard plowed on. Listening off to one side of the well-oiled crowd, Jim Smith was appalled.

"I'm going 'Holy shit, that stuff is mean! That isn't funny, it's just mean!'" he recalled. "He just changed the tenor (of the room)... that was pretty much the end of the party."

". . . I thought it was pretty brutal," agreed Dennis Rasmussen, the former Baltimore County executive. "It (was) over the top. But I suspect if the roles were reversed, Ed would have taken it just as far as Buzzy. And enjoyed every second of it."

For his part, Ed Hale never stopped smiling throughout the evening, no matter what manner of ragging was hurled his way.

In a few months, the lights in the penthouse would be turned off and the doors padlocked, and Hale would be looking for new place to hang his hat.

But if this was to be the last big blow-out, Ed Hale, as usual, was going out in style.

# CHAPTER 19

## The Fixer

By 2006, Ed Hale's public profile in Baltimore was at its most luminous. He was wealthier than ever and the Canton Crossing deal and tower project had solidified his reputation as one of the state's most prominent and influential tycoons.

Even more than before, a steady parade of ordinary citizens, developers and politicians appeared at his office door, seeking advice or favors. At times, it resembled the classic opening scene in "The Godfather," where a line of supplicants waited for an audience with Don Vito Corleone on the day of his daughter's wedding.

"People would come in all day: 'I just want five minutes of your time,'" Hale recalled. "They'd ask: 'What do you think I ought to do with this?' or 'Should I buy this company?' or "What do you think of this person?' 'Cause they thought I was a good judge of character."

One who turned to Hale for counsel was a local businessman seeking the best way to break off a relationship with a woman he'd been seeing for some time. ("He was a male 'Dear Abby!'" Hale's secretary, Cindy Smith, noted of her boss).

Another who sought guidance was Bernadette Gietka, a Dundalk woman and post office letter carrier who had just won the

$183-million Mega Millions lottery jackpot, the fourth largest in state history.

"Get really good advisors, people you can really trust," Hale told her, steering her to a financial consultant he considered among the best in the business.

At a Baltimore Ravens game when he was a guest of team owner Art Modell, Hale was approached by Ben Carson, the noted director of pediatric neurosurgery at The Johns Hopkins Hospital. Carson had just made money on a real estate deal and was seeking advice on how to invest it.

Hale felt honored to meet the world-famous surgeon and passed along a few tips. A few days later, he was invited to Carson's house, where the two men talked investing, shot pool and played Wii tennis.

Hale's connections in business and industry were so vast that when Sen. Barbara Mikulski and former Georgia senator Sam Nunn wanted to meet the new governor of Hong Kong, Mikulski asked Hale to arrange the sit-down.

No problem, Hale said. After all, the new governor was none other than C.H. Tung, former chairman of Orient Overseas Container Line, whom Hale had done business with years earlier.

What Hale facilitated most of all, however, were loans from 1st Mariner Bank—billions of dollars in loans. His loan committee would meet promptly at 11 a.m. every Thursday, and Hale made it a point to be there to sign off on each and every big-money loan.

At the time, he noted, many ordinary citizens "couldn't go to the blue-blood banks. They wouldn't approve you for a loan because they didn't like how you looked or dressed or acted. I wanted to give everybody a shot who didn't have a shot in other places."

Hale was also becoming a must-see figure for politicians, who increasingly turned to him for both his blessing and financial support.

"I was a fund-raiser, a bundler," Hale would say years later. "I arranged things. I would exert my influence whenever I could to raise funds for candidates I thought were good."

He started a PAC (political action committee) at 1st Mariner that allowed the bank's employees to voluntarily have portions of their paycheck deducted to support candidates Hale deemed worthy—often candidates sympathetic to the banking industry.

At its height, some 200 of the bank's 700 employees contributed on a regular basis to the PAC.

"Again, they were trusting my judgment," Hale said. "What was good for the bank was good for them and their career, in terms of backing the right people. I have a rule: I don't back anyone who's going to lose. I back a winner."

Like any savvy businessman, however, he would sometimes hedge his bets, especially in heated political races that were simply too close to call.

But this was not always greatly appreciated, as Hale discovered first-hand in 2006, when he was invited to dinner at the governor's mansion in Annapolis by then-Gov. Robert L. Ehrlich.

Ehrlich was running unopposed on the Republican ticket for a second term, while Martin O'Malley, the mayor of Baltimore, and Doug Duncan, the County Executive for Montgomery County, were the main rivals for the Democratic Party nod in the upcoming primary.

After the dinner party, as the guests—including new Ravens owner, Steve Bisciotti and various bank officers from Wachovia—were leaving, Kendall Ehrlich, the governor's wife, upbraided Hale.

"In front of everyone, she said: 'I have a bone to pick with you, Ed Hale,'" Hale recalled. "'You gave money to KKT.'"

Hale was stunned. The reference, he knew, was to $2,000 that he had given to the campaign of Kathleen Kennedy Townsend four years earlier. Kennedy had been Ehrlich's Democratic opponent in his first race for governor, and had lost narrowly.

Of course, as was his practice, Hale had also raised $44,000 at a fundraiser for Ehrlich in that same 2002 campaign.

Now, with Kendall Ehrlich confronting him in front of the other guests, Hale admitted contributing to KKT's coffers.

"But I gave your husband a lot more than that," he continued. "I hedge my bets because that's what I do. I'll tell you something else: I'm going to give money to Martin O'Malley. And I'm the treasurer for Ben Cardin's campaign—he's running for the Senate, it'll be announced in a couple of days.

"In case you didn't know it or realize it," Hale continued, with the governor now listening in, "if your husband wins, Martin O'Malley is still going to be the mayor for two more years. So what do you expect me to do?"

"I thought you were our friend," Hale recalls Kendal Ehrlich replying.

From there, Hale says now, the conversation rapidly devolved into Kendall Ehrlich offering to bet that Doug Duncan would beat O'Malley in the primary, and Hale accepting the wager simply to defuse the situation.

The next day, Hale received a phone call from Dick Hug, the governor's chief fundraiser. Kendall Ehrlich, Hug said, was still mighty steamed at what she viewed as Hale's betrayal.

By now, however, Hale was just as angry at Maryland's First Lady, whom he felt had gone out of her way to embarrass him the previous night.

"Let me make this easy for you," Hale told Hug. "I was going to hedge my bets and give some money to Martin O'Malley and some to Bob Ehrlich. Now I'm giving Bob zero."

From that point on, Hale's relationship with the Ehrlichs was effectively over. But over the years, most Maryland politicians were thrilled and grateful to have Ed Hale's imprimatur—no matter what form it took—on their campaigns.

Not long after O'Malley was elected governor in 2007, he and his wife, Judge Katie Curran O'Malley, appointed Hale to be the head of the decorating committee for Government House, the official name for the governor's mansion.

The businessman's first bit of advice?

Don't decorate.

"With the economy going in the tank the way it is," Hale told the O'Malleys, "I believe your timing couldn't be worse to go out now and let everyone know that you're redecorating the place."

The O'Malleys listened to Hale and left the mansion as it was. In the gathering gloom of the Great Recession, it proved to be just the right advice.

Then again, politicos had been listening to Ed Hale seemingly forever, dating back to his early years in trucking and shipping, when he'd emerged as a forceful—if callow—captain of industry.

William Donald Schaefer, then the mayor of Baltimore, had valued Hale's judgment to such an extent that he would routinely ask the young mogul to help screen candidates for office.

On one such occasion, Schaefer asked Hale to talk to a judge named Joseph F. Murphy Jr., who was being considered for the Court of Special Appeals.

Hale ended up vouching for Murphy and his character—even though Murphy had ruled against Hale's Port East Transfer in an accident case years earlier. Like many who had been the beneficiary of Hale's help, Murphy had never forgotten the kindness.

At a dinner years later for Baltimore lawyers and judges at the Maryland Club, as Hale was being introduced as the keynote speaker, Murphy, then the Chief Judge of the Court of Special Appeals, stood and delivered a few impromptu remarks.

He spoke movingly of his friendship with Hale, and of how the banking magnate did business and treated his employees at 1st Mariner.

Then he concluded: "I do not believe I would have been

appointed to the Court of Special Appeals without Ed's help. Ed's support was very, very important."

Listening to this amid the packed audience of prominent attorneys and jurists, Hale could only marvel at how far he'd come.

"It was one of the highlights of my life," he'd say years later of Murphy's touching tribute. "Coming from where I'm from, it was pretty heady stuff."

# CHAPTER 20

## Storm Clouds on the Horizon

By 2006, 1st Mariner Bank was an unequivocal success story, with $1.3 billion in assets and a stock price of slightly more than $20 a share.

As the chairman and CEO of Baltimore's largest independent bank, Ed Hale was enjoying the good times, starring in commercials with the Ravens' star quarterback, Joe Flacco, and basking in the seemingly endless good-will that his "hometown bank" was generating across the region.

But the upbeat mood was about to change in a dizzying sequence of events that no one saw coming.

In July, the bank's president, George Mantakos, called Hale into his office.

"Look at this," Mantakos said, a note of concern in his voice.

He opened a pair of folders on his desk. As Hale examined them, the only thing missing was ominous background music.

The folders contained two loans 1st Mariner had sold to Bear Stearns, the big New York investment bank. The borrowers had defaulted on the loans. Now Bear Stearns had sent them back to 1st Mariner under a buyer's remorse clause.

Hale was stunned at first. How had this happened?

He had never been crazy about the mortgage business in the first place, feeling it was, at best, a secondary business for the bank to be in and too volatile for his comfort. But mortgages, he realized, generated enough fee income and new customers to assume the risk.

The cause of the problem quickly became apparent: the bank, mainly its Northern Virginia division, was processing mortgages that required little or no documentation of a borrower's finances. These so called "liar loans" or "no-doc loans" were now being sent back by Bear Stearns.

Mantakos had already heard that some 10 loans were coming back. But those loans, the bank president would soon learn, "were just the tip of the iceberg."

Hearing this, Hale went from being stunned to being furious. And it was Brett Carter, the head of the bank's mortgage company, who bore the brunt of his ire.

"I would ask Brett Carter at every other board meeting: 'Are you sure we're not getting these loans back?'" Hale recalled. "And he'd assure me we weren't."

"It was Ed's impression always that these loans were sold and could never be returned to us," Mantakos says now. ". . .To me, Brett seemed like a straight shooter and he's been in the mortgage businesses 25 years. Maybe he (thought) the documentation was: once you buy it, it's yours. And you're buying it as is. But the documentation didn't support that."

Whoever was to blame, the losses mounted quickly for 1st Mariner. Eventually some $80 million in mortgages came back, costing the bank around $60 million.

"So what was a trickle," Hale recalled, "became a torrent."

In those heady, pre-recession days, the loan business was like the Wild West, with a semi-lawless, anything-goes feel that contributed to the bank's bleeding.

"Today you have to show the size of your underpants to get a loan," Hale says. "But no one was checking back then to see if these people were creditworthy, if they had the means to pay back loans.

"Back in those days, all you had to say was: 'My name is so-and-so and I make $90,000' and that's all you needed to do. There was no due diligence, no under-writing."

By 2008, with the economy tanking, the losses worsened. Bear Stearns and Lehman Brothers, the fourth-largest investment bank in the world, collapsed. An accounting scandal had AIG, the multi-national insurance giant, on the ropes. The U.S. housing market was gutted in the recession. Capital markets dried up quickly.

All of it affected 1st Mariner's fortunes, and the worry lines on Ed Hale's tanned face deepened.

The situation became increasingly dire. Due to the heavy volume of loans coming back, the bank failed to qualify for TARP, the Troubled Asset Relief Program implemented by the government to strengthen financial institutions.

In September of 2009, federal regulators slapped a "cease and desist" order on the bank. "That's like you're swimming to shore and they throw you an anchor," Hale says with a derisive snort

The order meant the bank was now mandated to come up with a plan to improve its capital, liquidity and earnings. It was also ordered to come up with a solution for its problem loans. Otherwise it could be directed to find a merger partner or even placed in receivership.

Outwardly, Hale professed confidence in his ability to get the bank out of the jam. Hadn't he pulled off a similar feat years earlier after taking over the Bank of Baltimore, when regulators were baying at his heels and he knew far less about the banking business?

Sure, he had. But inwardly he knew the bleak economic climate and the worst credit market in years would make things much tougher this time around.

"I didn't know what we were going to do, how we were going to do it," Hale recalled. "I was extremely worried."

Shareholders were beginning to howl. Many blamed Hale for the mess. How, they asked, could the bank's CEO *not* know the terms of the loans his bank was selling? Others wondered whether Hale's other business interests were keeping him from focusing on the bank and giving this looming crisis the immediate and total attention it deserved.

"He was in a very bad situation, and it was taking its toll on him," said Jennifer Gilbert, his ex-girlfriend, who had stayed in contact with him. ". . . But in Ed Hale fashion, he saw a way out. He was plotting and planning and strategizing. ...And it wasn't pretty and it wasn't pleasant.

"In some ways, though, I think when you start with nothing, the fear of going back to nothing maybe isn't as great," she continued. "Because you know you did it once and you can do it again. You can pull yourself out."

Desperate to raise cash, Hale hit on the idea of launching an all-out grass-roots effort aimed at some of 1st Mariner's most loyal customers. He arranged a series of meetings in the region with individual investors, hoping to get them to buy stock in the bank so it could continue to operate.

The first of these events was held at Squires Italian Restaurant in Dundalk in the spring of 2010. In the audience were teachers, ironworkers, small business owners, retirees and a smattering of seasoned investors who had made money when Hale ran the Bank of Baltimore, and who hoped he could work his magic again.

Also on hand were Carol Hale and a number of her friends. As the audience enjoyed a modest spread of pepperoni pizza, beer and soda, Hale went into his pitch.

He made no attempt to minimize the severity of the problem.

"Ed was very careful that people understood the bank was in trouble," Mantakos said.

"I would stand there," Hale recalled, "and tell them all: 'This is not for the faint of heart.'"

But in appealing for investors, he also emphasized what an important role the bank played in the local community, and how different it was from the cold, faceless financial entities they'd once dealt with that didn't give a damn about their needs.

Watching Hale work the room from a nearby table, Mantakos could see that his boss's message resonated immediately with the crowd.

"This was the Dundalk community," Mantakos said. "His *mom* was there! It was a love-fest! No matter what he said, they were going to take it away as a positive event. And they felt—and rightly so, probably—'He's being honest with us. The bank's in trouble. It's Ed, and if he thinks he's going to turn it around, we're going to help him.'"

In the end, the evening was a resounding success. Plenty of audience members reached for their checkbooks and Hale raised far more money than he'd anticipated. But the event also proved sobering in some ways for the embattled bank chairman and CEO.

"It was gratifying," he recalled, "but I had a heavy, heavy responsibility. These people were going to put in $1500 or $150 or whatever it was, and it was so meaningful to them. Maybe this was money they were going to use for their medications, but they were going to put it here because it was a good investment.

"The thing I was struck by," he went on, "was that some of the people who put the money up didn't even know what a share of stock meant. They didn't understand this. All they understood was that it was me asking. These were people from my neighborhood. They were thinking: If Ed Hale's doing it, it's got to be good."

Hale went on to hold similar fund-raisers in Pikesville, Towson, Annapolis and Bel Air, among other locales, receiving enthusiastic responses each time from investors.

At the Sheraton hotel in Annapolis, a retired U.S. Marine Corps general rose halfway through Hale's spiel and said: "I'm telling you right now, sir, I'm going to put my money in to do this. Because these robbers that are at these other banks, I don't trust them. I trust a man like you."

All told, Hale would go on to raise $10.7 million. The figure astounded the New York advisory firm of Sandler O'Neill, which had been hired by the bank to come up with ideas for raising capital and whose executives had sniffed at Hale's populist fund-raising effort.

"They told me: 'You'll never get it done,'" Hale recalled.

But he had. It wasn't easy and it wasn't pretty, he told everyone. But it was done.

The money he'd raised gave the bank some breathing room. Hale had put up $2 million of his own money and the bank had sold its consumer finance unit for another $14.5 million.

Now he began making plans to embark with hat in hand on so-called "road shows" to the big Manhattan investment banks to raise even more revenue.

But early in 2011, 1st Mariner reached a tentative deal with the New York investment firm Priam Capital that would change everything. The firm agreed to give the bank $36 million for a 25 per cent stake in the company if 1st Mariner could raise $124 million in additional revenue.

At a lunch one month earlier with Howard Feinglass, a Baltimore native who was Priam's managing director, Hale discovered that his days as bank chairman and CEO were numbered.

The two met at the Dockside Restaurant in Canton, a stone's throw from the 1st Mariner Tower. Hale was immediately put off by Feinglass' distracted manner: the other man constantly checked his iPad and made little eye contact as they talked.

When the food arrived, Hale watched in semi-horror as Feinglass proceeded to mash his potato into a pulpy mess with his fork and smother it with ketchup.

But as preoccupied as the Priam honcho seemed, there was no mistaking his message when he eventually got around to it.

"He told me he was going to cleanse the bank of management and bring in his own people," Hale remembered. "I said 'Fine.' I never changed my expression. But I was bristling inside."

He was also stunned that Priam and Feinglass wouldn't want him to stay on in some capacity, even though there had been talk of Hale possibly assuming a "non-executive chairman" role.

"I thought: what kind of egotistical fool was this guy not to use me?" Hale recalled. "I'm *known* around Baltimore, with all the marketing that had been done for the bank. I had such a great relationship with people. You could capitalize on what I bring to the table and the institutional knowledge I had.

"If you were going to bring in the upper-crust guys to run things," he continued, referring to the old-line Mercantile Bank and Trust executives who were part of the group of investors with Priam—"why not maintain the relationship I had with the blue-collar customers?"

Around this time, Martin O'Malley and his two sons visited Hale at his Talbot County farm.

The two boys and their dad, now the governor, had a great time boating with Hale on Hunting Creek, a tributary of the Miles River. They also rode four-wheelers on the lush, picturesque grounds that curl around the water.

But the governor had been following the media accounts of 1st Mariner's troubles closely, and he sensed that the whole business was weighing heavily on Hale that day.

"It was a time," O'Malley recalled, "when I suspect he was lower than whale shit. (But) he was stoic, licking his wounds... he'd been knocked pretty hard on the solar plexus. First and foremost on his mind was the lives of his employees... he was going to continue to do whatever he could to make the best deal . . .to save as many employees as he could.

During the entire ordeal, O'Malley continued, "He never asked me to give him a free pass or to ask the regulators to leave him alone. We were watching as this whole thing happened, too."

Initial news reports suggested that 1st Mariner's deal with Priam was contingent upon Hale resigning as chairman and CEO once the transaction was completed. But Hale later insisted that wasn't the case.

The real story, he said, was this: he had turned 65 in November of that year. And with no clearly-defined role being offered by the Priam people, he reluctantly decided to step down as part of a plan to reduce his taxes, something he'd thought about for months.

The strategy called for him sell 1 million shares of bank stock at a loss to offset big gains he had realized on a real estate sale. But bank policy required him to step down in order to sell the shares.

So on Dec. 22, 2011, Ed Hale resigned with a heavy heart from the bank he had founded and nurtured for the better part of 16 years.

The bank had lost some $120 million over the previous four years. It had been in the red for 18 straight quarters. Hale, too, had taken a financial drubbing—the worst of his career. Although his salary as the head of the bank had been $540,000 and he was the company's largest shareholder by far, he had lost a staggering $44 million when the stock price cratered.

That evening, Hale was visited at his Miller's Island home by his old friend, Bonnie Fleck. Fleck was a Realtor for Coldwell Banker who had helped with the sale of Hale's Anchorage Tower condo. Now, she had dropped by to console him.

She found him in the kitchen, looking drained.

"I know it's been a rough day," she said, giving him a hug.

"You have no idea," Hale replied. "I've just been eating shit all day."

The two drank a beer and eventually went out to dinner at a local restaurant.

"What should we have?" Hale asked when they were seated and had opened their menus.

"Why not shit on a shingle?" Fleck replied. "You said you've been eating shit all day."

Hale laughed. For the next few minutes, the two went back and forth, working the s-word into every dish they could think of until both were howling. When she left Hale a couple of hours later at the restaurant, she could see his spirits had lifted and some of his old resolve had returned.

Five days later, Ed Hale would repay Fleck's kindness—and then some.

That morning, he called and asked her to meet him at the Dockside Restaurant for lunch. Once they'd sat down, he asked if she was interested in buying 500,000 shares of his bank stock at two cents a share, for a total of $10,000.

The selling off of his stock was about to begin in earnest.

Fleck was divorced after 28 years of marriage and her mother, Catherine Nash, was dying and under hospice care. The Realtor didn't know about the high drama Ed Hale was involved in at the bank or anything about the tax strategy he was trying to implement—nor did he enlighten her.

But she sensed that Hale was offering her an incredible opportunity to buy stock at a ridiculously-low price. And she trusted her friend implicitly.

Studying him, she nodded and said: "You wouldn't ask me to do something that was not beneficial to me."

"I appreciate that," was all Hale said.

Two days later, Bonnie Fleck signed the paperwork and the deal was done. It would prove to be a wildly fortuitous decision on her part.

"It was a leap of faith," she would say three years later. "(But) let me tell you, those shares of stock made me a millionaire at some point. They kept going up, to $2.97 a share, they kept going up. I was able to pay off my condo, buy a house from my sister, and pay off every bill I ever had. It changed my life."

After resigning from 1st Mariner, Hale told the media that his short-term plans were to spend the next few months hunting on his farm, enjoying the rest of the Blast season and devoting more attention to his real estate holdings at the site near the 1st Mariner Tower where the proposed Shops at Canton Crossing were being developed.

But surprising absolutely no one, Hale did not step down quietly. He still saw himself as the ultimate outsider in the stuffy world of the banking Brahmans, the Dundalk guy with the rough edges who would forever be held at arm's length by the city's elite movers and shakers.

He was down, sure, but far from out. The bluster was still there, simmering just below the surface as always.

So when a banking analyst named Bert Ely was quoted in the *Sun* as saying 1st Mariner would have been better off if Hale had left years earlier and reporters sought him out for a comment, Ed Hale did not mince words.

"Tell him," he replied tartly, "he can kiss my ass."

# CHAPTER 21

## "The Deepest, Darkest Bowl of Crap."

Ed Hale has always described late September 2009 as "the worst time of my life." No one who was around him during that grim period would accuse him of hyperbole, either.

Just days after 1st Mariner Bank was slapped with a "cease-and desist" order to boost capital and fix problem loans, Hale was hit with another body blow: a French bank announced that it had begun foreclosure proceedings on his beloved 1st Mariner Tower.

An October auction for the 17-story building was scheduled by Paris-based Natixis, a corporate and investment bank, after what it said was the default on an $84 million loan

The news caused a furor in the Baltimore media. As soon as the word leaked out, helicopters from area TV stations began buzzing around the tower and reporters from the local newspapers descended on Hale's office.

The media narrative being shaped was clear: Ed Hale was really on the ropes this time.

Fall-out from the Great Recession, which had damaged economies across the globe, was about to cripple his commercial real estate business in much the same way as it had his bank. Sure, he was a wily businessman who had survived tough times in the past. But how in God's name was he going to get out of this predicament?

Even though he was still in shock, Hale appeared stoic when he faced the media a few days later.

He was current on the tower loan, he explained. But Natixis had decided not to renew it because he was in default on a couple of provisions. The major problem was a Utility Distribution Center he'd built to supply power to Canton Crossing tenants; the bank was concerned that he was paying too much to finance the project.

Yes, Hale admitted, this foreclosure business didn't look good, especially coming on the heels of the bank's "cease-and-desist" order. And with the lending markets practically dried up—especially for individual developers—getting a new loan was definitely going to be a challenge.

"I'm going to do what I have to do here," Hale told the *Sun*. "I'm going to list the building for sale. I'm going to continue to talk to people about refinancing it, and just look at all the alternatives."

Of Natixis, he added: "They're sticking it to me." Then after a sigh: "I don't know how much more they can."

Hale was proud of his role in developing the signature tower and prouder still that it had maintained a nearly-full occupancy rate the past three years, with a positive cash flow. Although he had soured on his isolated life in his posh penthouse, the tower had proved to be a vibrant addition to the Canton waterfront and a source of pride for the people who worked in it, as well as for those who lived in the surrounding neighborhoods.

Indeed plans for a Main Street-style shopping center were still underway, and proposals for a pair of waterfront pavilions that would include shops and offices were also being discussed.

But everywhere he turned for financing help, he was rebuffed.

A $100 million deal with JP Morgan a year earlier had fallen through at the last minute when Hale was told the bank had suddenly dropped its commercial mortgage-backed securities division.

"That was an 'oh-shit' moment of a magnitude I can't even describe," he said. "That was a $100 million deal!"

After that he had begun scrambling for loans, looking to banks all over the country and in Europe for help.

"I was even going to fly to Dubai to meet with bankers there," he said.

Hale's lawyer, Michael Gallerizzo of the Baltimore law firm Gebhart & Smith, was urging him to declare Chapter 11 bankruptcy, saying the move would save the beleaguered banker and developer some $86 million.

But the idea was personally abhorrent to Hale, a man still convinced of his toughness and smarts and ability to wriggle out of any jam.

He also worried that once word got out about the bankruptcy—he envisioned a sensational front-page story in the Sun, with the kind of blaring headline not seen since the Sept. 11 attacks and "DEVASTATION!"—there would be a serious run on the bank. Especially given the recent "cease and desist" order.

"People would have been lining up to take their money out of the bank," he recalled of that time. "I said: 'I can't do that to them, I can't do it to the employees, I can't do it to all the investors and the bond-holders. I'm just not built that way.'"

But his options were dwindling rapidly.

Between the need to right his ailing bank and stave off foreclosure on his signature tower, Hale was under enormous pressure. Outwardly, he projected a business-as-usual demeanor. But those who knew him well could sense the toll the ordeal was taking on him.

"I don't know if he was ready to jump off the 17th floor of the tower or not—it wouldn't surprise me," George Mantakos says, shaking his head at the memory of that time. "If I came to work the next day and he was lying on the sidewalk, I wouldn't have been shocked.

"I would have been hurt, but I wouldn't have been shocked. He was under suicidal pressure. There's no doubt about it. I don't know how he survived it."

At 1st Mariner Bank, some who watched Ed Hale drag himself into work every day came to see him as a doomed figure, like the lone sheriff in the Old West movies about to face the murderous outlaw gang at sun-up.

"We have no idea how he was able to go to sleep and wake up every morning," said Ken Jones, at the time a facilities manager for the bank. "I mean, it was awful! It was absolutely awful! The *stress*. The *tension*. A lot of people would have either put a gun in their mouth or jumped off the roof of a building.

"But he's a tough guy," Jones added. "They don't come any tougher than Ed."

Buzzy Krongard had always marveled at his friend's ability to avert disaster, and he, too, had used a movie analogy to explain it.

"In a sense," Krongard said, "it's like watching one of the old westerns and the guy drops off a cliff and then suddenly he's hanging from a tree branch." Instead of being a tiny red splat mark on the canyon floor hundreds of feet below.

Years later, Hale would say what kept him going as 1st Mariner floundered and the tower crisis loomed was this: the stakes were simply too high for him to crumple.

"I knew I had to stand tall and figure a way out of this," Hale said. "There were too many jobs at stake, too many lives would have been disrupted if I didn't. I just kept telling myself: 'Don't get lazy. Don't give in to the depression. Just stand tall.'"

Yet Hale was also, above all else, a realist. After months and months of looking for financing help, he finally concluded that none would be forthcoming.

Faced with no other choice, he agreed to sell the building for $125 million to Corporate Office Properties Trust (COPT), a

Columbia development company that had a second mortgage on the tower.

The closing took place in the board room of the Constellation Energy building in Baltimore. Surrounded by stacks of documents and a small army of lawyers droning on and on, an exhausted, dispirited Ed Hale felt as if his head were about to explode as the deal was hammered out.

Hale had planned to grab a late dinner after the closing and, as was his custom when he walked the streets of the city at night, he was carrying a weapon.

"It's 10 at night and I've *had* it," Hale recalled. "I have my .357 Magnum on my ankle. And at one point I looked at Mike Gallerizzo and I joked: 'Settle this or I'm gonna go off like Yosemite Sam here. Make it *end*!'"

Moments before the closing became official, Gallerizzo urged him one last time to consider declaring bankruptcy.

"No, I have no choice," Hale replied sharply. "We're moving forward. Let's stop talking about it."

When the lawyers finally *did* stop talking and all the papers were signed and Hale walked out into the night, the magnitude of the entire ordeal smacked him in the face.

Yes, he had avoided foreclosure. But the price was steep. COPT had originally offered him $100 million for the tower, and by strategically considering bankruptcy, he had ended up with another $25 million. But given all the money he'd put into the tower's construction, he'd actually suffered a cash loss of some $20 million.

Still, his close friends and associates marveled at how well the strategy had worked.

"I don't know how he got *any* money out of the tower," Mantakos says, shaking his head. "If I was the banker in the tower, he would have gotten nothing and I would have sued him. I don't know how he did it.

Mantakos laughs and shakes his head again. "I was *there* and I don't know how he did it."

But the boldness of the move—and how well thought out it was—was fully in keeping with Ed Hale's persona, said many of his friends.

In the weeks when negotiations for the tower were being hammered out, Hale had instructed his secretary, Cindy Smith, to tell callers to his office that he was unavailable, due to the fact that he was meeting with lawyers in Annapolis.

Although Smith never spelled out exactly what kind of lawyers he was huddling with, Hale hoped the COPT people would deduce they were bankruptcy specialists, and that he was panicking and running for the hills.

In the end, the strategy had worked well enough to save him $25 million. And that money could at least help him start digging out of a mountain of debt.

"Over all the years that I've known Ed," Ken Jones would say later, "he could fall from the highest heights into the deepest, darkest bowl of crap. And when he comes out, he's gonna be all right. It's just Ed. It's just his nature."

The saddest chapter in Ed Hale's life was now officially over. The iconic tower with the signature green roof now belonged to a publicly-traded office development company based in Howard County.

But after all the machinations he'd performed to hold onto the tower, the man who had dreamed it and built it could live with that.

"I don't ever have to worry about my legacy—*ever*," Hale would say fiercely. "Because for 100 years, that building is going to be there."

# CHAPTER 22

## Still Going for the Action

Following his departure from troubled 1st Mariner Bank, Ed Hale spent the first few weeks hunting and focusing on the Blast after his induction into the Major Indoor Soccer League Hall of Fame a few months earlier.

In a January 2012 interview with the *Sun*, he said he was "downshifting" to another phase of his life. At some point, he told the newspaper, he would be "happy or relieved" to have left the bank and all its attendant problems.

But he wasn't there yet, he admitted. And he had no plans to retire.

Those who knew him well also knew this: there were only so many geese he could blast out of the skies and so much attention he could give his soccer team before he'd begin to chafe at no longer being a Master of the Universe, at being sidelined from the corporate wheeling and dealing that had been his métier for so long.

The idea of cutting ties with the bank he'd conceived and nurtured for so many years was also hard to swallow. To imagine 1st Mariner without Ed Hale, the public face of the company, was as unthinkable to him as it was to so many of the bank's employees and customers.

"The bank was *my* idea!" he would say heatedly. "It wasn't the board of directors' idea. I put them in there. It was *my* baby! I thought of it. I implemented it. I got the money together. People listened to me. I raised the capital to start it. I put my own money in."

At 65, Hale was convinced that he was still at the top of his game, as sharp and business-savvy as ever. And it puzzled him as to why the new people running the bank couldn't see that, too, why they wouldn't lean on him for advice and counsel.

But he knew there would be no going back to 1st Mariner.

For one thing, he had doubts about whether the Priam Capital people brought in to rescue the bank could actually pull off the feat. He also felt alienated from the board of directors, whom he felt had failed to support him as he feverishly looked for ways to stop the bank's bleeding.

Finally, he was also troubled that the bank was now considering filing for bankruptcy. There were, in his view, other less-onerous ways to nurse it back to financial health.

When he'd left 1st Mariner in December of 2011, he and other officials had done virtually everything possible to cut spending and shrink the balance sheet by not adding more loans and working out bad loans, as well as by trimming staff, mainly through attrition.

And when the bank posted an impressive first quarter in 2012, fueled by a surge in residential mortgages, Hale was indignant that bankruptcy still seemed in the plans.

"I'm thinking: this is not right!" he said. "The company is making money! We don't have to go into a bankruptcy like this. We can do some re-structuring. Why throw in the towel? It's not my nature to quit. It's *not*. And everybody will tell you that.

"I survived all kind of crap. And I was not going to throw in the towel on this."

Bankruptcy, he knew, would effectively wipe out shareholder

gains and hurt the hundreds of investors who had rallied to his side and bought 1st Mariner stock during his grass-roots fund-raising drive.

There was also, to be sure, a personal financial interest at stake. As the majority shareholder with 1.3 million shares, Hale, too, would feel the pain of a bankruptcy-triggered stock loss.

But as he thought about all the good-hearted folks of modest means—many from his own Dundalk community—who had opened their hearts and their pocketbooks to him, Hale, not a religious man, recalled the Biblical sermon of the Widow's Offering.

In it, Jesus is watching the rich people putting money in the temple offering box when He sees a poor widow in rags put in two small copper coins.

Gathering his disciples, Jesus says: "Truly, I say to you, this poor widow has put in more than all of those who are contributing to the offering box. For they all contributed out of their abundance, but she out of her poverty has put in everything she had, all she had to live on."

The passage hit home with Hale, he said, "because I knew I could afford to lose the money, and that a lot of those other people couldn't. And I felt bad about that. I felt I had let people down. That's why I really wasn't giving up."

Over time, he had crafted an ambitious, complex plan to help the bank regain its financial footing, a plan the new board had repeatedly rejected. But in May, on his own dime, Hale launched another last-ditch effort. He traveled by train to New York for a meeting with David R. Seligman, a partner with the law firm Kirkland & Ellis and a specialist in corporate restructuring and insolvency proceedings.

Hale had brought in Kirkland & Ellis months earlier to try to work out a deal with the bank's debt holders, because there were interest payments on debt that were due. Now in Manhattan he spoke with Seligman and Vik Ghei, a young, well-respected financial consultant representing those same debt holders.

Hale laid out a new version of his plan, which consisted of three key components:

No. 1, he would offer the debt-holders a debt-for-equity deal that would eliminate some $50 million of debt. No. 2, he would have to raise capital, a figure somewhere between $60 and $100 million.

And no. 3, by doing this and maintaining a majority share, bank officials would trigger deferred tax assets worth some $40 million.

"To me, the company would have been worth $120 million," he said. "That is a quantum leap from being underwater at the time by like $10 million."

At the end of the meeting, Hale received assurances from Seligman and Ghei that the plan was plausible.

"It was not without its problems legally, organizationally and with regulators," Hale admitted. "But it was possible to (implement) with a lot of hard work. And I was ready to do that."

Excited at having this new strategy blessed by the two financial heavyweights, Hale rode back to Baltimore. But the board's response to this new strategy was still tepid.

Part of the reason, Hale felt, was that the board was under the sway of an attorney named Gary Bronstein of Kilpatrick Townsend & Stockton. This was another law firm, based in Washington, D.C., that had been brought in to help the bank out of its financial mess.

And while Hale found Bronstein to be an affable-enough fellow, he had nicknamed him "Chicken Little" for his lack of innovative ideas and unwillingness to take bold, decisive action to save the bank.

Time after time over the next four months, Hale would ask the board members: "Why are you not embracing this?"

Each time, he failed to receive a firm answer. Word eventually got back to him, however, that some board members doubted he could raise the necessary capital—even though that had been one of his true talents in the past.

Hoping to convince the board, Hale took it upon himself to begin contacting investment bankers, hedge funds, private equity firms and well-heeled individual investors such as Peter G. Angelos, the renowned Baltimore attorney and owner of the Baltimore Orioles, in an attempt to raise money quickly.

Sandler O'Neill, a New York investment banking firm, had been hired by 1st Mariner to facilitate these "road-show" bids to raise cash. A member of the firm named Ed Stein was brought in to coach Hale on how to speak to potential investors.

But Hale promptly became disillusioned with Stein's guidance. He considered Stein incompetent and quickly nicknamed him "Pig Vomit" after the character in the movie "Private Parts" that starred Howard Stern.

Hale had just set up a fund-raising trip to San Diego, Chicago and New York in mid-September of 2013 when he pulled up to his Rosedale office one morning and his cell phone rang.

On the other end were two senior 1st Mariner executives. Skipping the customary pleasantries, they got right to the bad news.

The two execs told Hale they had just gotten off the phone with the Federal Reserve.

"They said under no circumstances would they take anything I had in terms of a deal," Hale remembered. "This plan that I had in motion was dead. Not only would they not consider this plan, they wouldn't take any of the investors that I had lined up, either."

After hanging up, Hale sat in his car, the silence enveloping him as the finality of his mission sunk in.

"I was hit with a baseball bat, *WHAM!* I had done everything I could at my own expense," he said. "I spent probably $300,000 to $400,000 just to get to that point, and I expected to be reimbursed if I was successful. I had accountants, lawyers and investment bankers lined up. I was ready to go. But that phone call was the end."

The rejection was a devastating blow to a proud man for whom "We built this bank for you" was not just another empty advertising slogan or cheesy motto to be hung on a plaque behind his desk.

But within weeks, another monument to Hale's vision appeared with the October grand opening of the $105 million shopping center on Boston Street called The Shops at Canton Crossing.

At the ribbon-cutting ceremony, with bands playing and school children singing and some 500 people in attendance, including such dignitaries as Lt. Governor Anthony Brown and Baltimore Mayor Stephanie Rawlings-Blake, city councilman Jim Kraft took the microphone.

After heaping lavish praise on the developers, the Chesapeake Real Estate Group, and thanking them for all their hard work, Kraft told the crowd: "But we wouldn't be here today if it weren't for Ed Hale."

The man himself, though, was nowhere in sight.

He had elected to skip the event, telling everyone that the spotlight belonged to Doug Schmidt and the other developers, not him. Instead, he spent the afternoon just 13 miles away at his home on Miller's Island.

Although coverage of the event was splashed all over the local news, Hale didn't watch a minute of it. Instead, he spent the afternoon working at a table in his living room, the giant TV nearby tuned soundlessly to the business channel CNBC.

Still, the satisfaction he derived from the mall's opening was immense. And the memories of his role in its creation came flooding back.

In the spring of 2005, Hale had made a deal with Exxon to lease the 31 acres that now housed the gleaming new Shops. He had originally envisioned using the land for parking for 1st Mariner Bank Tower. But three years later, Exxon offered to sell him the land and he leaped at the opportunity.

At this point, he thought he might develop the property himself, envisioning a shopping area along the lines of Faneuil Hall, the historic marketplace on the Boston waterfront that had become one of the most-visited tourist sites in the U.S.

That plan eventually fell through. But what followed was another shrewd business deal of the type Hale had been making all his adult life.

With a contract to purchase in hand, he worked out at an agreement with Exxon to clean up the gas-soaked site and secured $3.5 million in state funding to help. And in June of 2011, he sold the contract—for land he never officially owned, except for a nanosecond at closing - to the developer Chesapeake Real Estate Group for a whopping $14.7 million.

The deal netted Hale some $11.8 million after clean-up costs. Some regarded it as perhaps the best deal he'd ever made.

"It was the biggest frickin' flip in Maryland history!" marvels Ken Jones to this day.

Now, three years after the closing, on a bleak site formerly overrun by weeds, gravel pits, chemical waste and giant feral cats, a gleaming new urban mall had opened with 30 shops and restaurants, including a 135,000-square-foot Target and a big Harris Teeter supermarket set to join them.

Finally, there was a place in Canton to buy towels—and anything else anyone could want. And none of it, the developers agreed, would have happened without Hale's foresight.

"He's kind of a nut," Doug Schmidt would say of Hale a few months after the grand opening. "So what he saw down there, people said 'You're crazy.' And maybe they were right. But whether it was luck or time or fortune or whatever, he did stuff that people thought he couldn't do.

"I give him all the credit for having the vision to do that."

As 2014 unfolded, it was clear that Ed Hale's days of wheeling and dealing were far from over.

That summer, he prepared to sell 2.78 acres of land behind the Shops at Canton Crossing to a developer who planned to build a 500-unit apartment complex on the site.

Hale had bought the property 20 years ago for $550,000. Now it was expected to fetch somewhere around $25 million.

"That's not too bad, is it?" he'd say with a grin.

The cocky grin told you everything you needed to know about Ed Hale. As did this: when a reporter from the *Baltimore Business Journal* called in August to ask whether Hale thought $25 million was a steep price to pay for a "swatch of undeveloped land," Hale responded: "That's your opinion. My opinion is that it's low."

No, there was plenty of life left in him, plenty of wheeling and dealing to be done before he retired to endless days of hunting and fishing and lazing about on his Talbot County farm.

For all who would listen, he had the same message: "I'm not done yet."

Anyone who thought otherwise was crazy.

# ED HALE'S LIFE LESSONS

1.  Don't be lazy. It's habit-forming.

2.  Observe the "No Dickheads" rule. Don't hang with people who are nasty, negative and take you down. Cut them out of your life. Dealing with jerks requires too much negative energy.

3.  Life is not a dress rehearsal. If people or things make you unhappy, move on.

4.  Take the advice of legendary frontiersman and Congressman Davy Crocket: "When you're sure you're right, then go ahead."

5.  Don't be a "woulda, coulda, shoulda" when it comes to things. When I hear that from people, I glaze over. "I coulda bought that for $100,000 and now it's worth $450,000." That's weak. Don't talk, do it.

6.  A hero dies once, a coward dies 10,000 times.

7.  Don't let people walk over you.

8.  Use your creative side all the time.

9.  Make a list of things to do and do them. Don't procrastinate

when things need to be done. They don't go away or get better with time.

10. Hire people smarter than you and manage them. If you surround yourself with friends and family, it's not going to work in business.

11. Work smart and put the time in. Bosses watch and so will employees.

12. Never rehire someone that leaves for greener pastures. Rarely, if ever, do they stay and work out.

13. Delegate. You can't do it all yourself.

14. Keep pressure up. Be relentless in all pursuits.

15. Follow up.

16. Try new things. Don't get into a rut with the same businesses and relationships.

17. Don't let people mistake kindness for weakness.

18. Revenge is fun.

19. There's a fine line between risk-taking and thrill-seeking.

20. You're as good as your last performance.

21. Get the facts and then make your decision.

22. Don't talk too much.

23. If the geese are coming, you don't have to call them. That applies to both waterfowl and people.

24. Learn new things all the time. Learn the tasks others around you do. You become more useful.

25. Be tough, but fair.

26. If you see a break, take it.

27. Start early and stay late if the job is not done. Be wise with your time.

28. Turn change into opportunity.

29. Be passionate and care.

30. Stay efficient so you can remain competitive.

31. Get customers and keep them for life.

32. Send handwritten personal notes. People still love to receive them.

33. Know your limitations in business and personal relationships.

34. Keep growing or the competition will overtake you.

35. Take the higher ground and be honest and blunt. It saves time.

36. Listen to people's opinions. Cut out the assholes. They suck up energy.

37. Praise people and don't look for praise about yourself. Spread compliments around.

38. Anticipate trends.

39. Price properly.

40. Give people what they want.

41. A deal isn't done until the green crosses the mahogany.

42. Personally, I like to give more than receive.

43. Humor is fun.

44. Play pranks and let people play them on you.

45. Don't lie—you spend too much time trying to remember what you said.

46. Old school is definitely good.

47. If you are a draw, volunteer to lead charitable events.

48. Jewish people do more in the morning in business, education, arts and charity than the "Blue Bloods" do all year. The Blue Bloods were born on third base and think they hit a triple.

49. Just do it!

50. Less is more.

51. Hire attitude over ability.

52. Enthusiasm!

53. Communicate, but don't over-do it.

54. Be punctual. At work, it's 90 percent of the deal just showing up on time.

55. Beat the boss to work. It leaves an impression.

56. Some of the best deals you make are the ones you don't.

57. Remember what Atilla the Hun said: "The chieftain doesn't eat and drink with the warriors."

58. Remember what Benjamin Franklin said: "Fish, family and friends stink after three days."

# AUTHOR'S BIOGRAPHY

Kevin Cowherd was an award-winning features and sports columnist for *The Baltimore Sun* for 32 years before taking a buyout in 2013. He is the co-author, along with Hall of Famer Cal Ripken Jr., of the *New York Times* best-seller "Hothead" and three other baseball novels for young readers.

He has also written for *Men's Health, Parenting* and *Baseball Digest* magazines and is the author of a collection of columns, "Last Call at the 7-Eleven," published by Bancroft Press.

He lives with his wife, Nancy, in Cockeysville, Md.

**Apprentice House Press**
*Loyola University Maryland*

Apprentice House is the country's only campus-based, student-staffed book publishing company. Directed by professors and industry professionals, it is a nonprofit activity of the Communication Department at Loyola University Maryland.

Using state-of-the-art technology and an experiential learning model of education, Apprentice House publishes books in untraditional ways. This dual responsibility as publishers and educators creates an unprecedented collaborative environment among faculty and students, while teaching tomorrow's editors, designers, and marketers.

Outside of class, progress on book projects is carried forth by the AH Book Publishing Club, a co-curricular campus organization supported by Loyola University Maryland's Office of Student Activities.

Eclectic and provocative, Apprentice House titles intend to entertain as well as spark dialogue on a variety of topics. Financial contributions to sustain the press's work are welcomed. Contributions are tax deductible to the fullest extent allowed by the IRS.

To learn more about Apprentice House books or to obtain submission guidelines, please visit www.apprenticehouse.com.

Apprentice House Press
Communication Department
Loyola University Maryland
4501 N. Charles Street
Baltimore, MD 21210
Ph: 410-617-5265 • Fax: 410-617-2198
info@apprenticehouse.com • www.apprenticehouse.com

CPSIA information can be obtained at www.ICGtesting.com
Printed in the USA
BVOW02*1903041214

377977BV00008B/60/P